Tübinger Beiträge zur Anglistik 9

Herausgegeben von Joerg O. Fichte
und Hans-Werner Ludwig

Joerg O. Fichte (ed.)

Chaucer's Frame Tales

The Physical and the Metaphysical

 Gunter Narr Verlag Tübingen
D.S. Brewer Cambridge

Cip-Kurztitelaufnahme der Deutschen Bibliothek

Chaucer's frame tales : the phys. and the metaphys. / Joerg O. Fichte (ed.) –
Tübingen : Narr, 1987.
  (Tübinger Beiträge zur Anglistik ; 9)
  ISBN 3-87808-329-7

NE: Fichte, Joerg O. [Hrsg.]; Chaucer, Geoffrey [Mitarb.]; GT

British Library Cataloguing in Publication Data

Chaucer's frame tales : the physical and metaphysical.
1. Chaucer, Geoffrey – Criticism and interpretation
I. Fichte, Joerg O.
821'.1   PR 1924
  ISBN 0-85991-235-3

Library of Congress Cataloging-in-Publication Data

Chaucer's frame tales. Contents: The origins of comicality in Chaucer /
Willi Erzgräber – Versions of comedy in Chaucer's Canterbury tales /
Derek Pearsall – Chaucer's Shipman's tale within the context of the French
fabliaux tradition / Joerg O. Fichte – [etc.]
1. Chaucer, Geoffrey, d. 1400-Technique. 2. Chaucer, Geoffrey, d. 1400.
Canterbury tales. 3. Frame-stories. I. Fichte, Jörg O.
PR1933.F7C48 1987   821'.1   86-29979
  ISBN 0-85991-235-3

Published in Great Britain by D. S. Brewer, 240 Hills Road, Cambridge
an imprint of Boydell & Brewer Ltd, P. O. Box 9, Woodbridge, Suffolk IP 12 3 DF.

© 1987 · Gunter Narr Verlag Tübingen
Alle Rechte vorbehalten. Nachdruck oder Vervielfältigung, auch
auszugsweise, in allen Formen wie Mikrofilm, Xerographie, Mikrofiche,
Mikrocard, Offset verboten.

Druck: Gulde-Druck, Tübingen
Printed in Germany

ISBN 3-87808-329-7 (Narr)
ISBN 0-85991-235-3 (Brewer)

Table of Contents

Preface

This collection of papers presents a mini-series of lectures given in Tübingen during the summer term of 1985 within the larger context of a lecture course on Chaucer's *Canterbury Tales*. Although the guest speakers were free to choose their topics, a remarkable unanimity of interests soon became apparent: four participants opted for a discussion of either Chaucerian comedy or the fabliaux. Despite this common interest, however, which for a moment baffled the organizer who was afraid that duplication might occur, the four speakers took different approaches to the subject they had chosen to investigate. In a fashion typical of contemporary Chaucer scholarship, many divergent views were presented on the same subject.

Thus, Willi Erzgräber bases his view of the "Origins of Comicality in Chaucer" on a statement by Karl-Heinz Stierle who defines the subject as follows: "Gegenstand des Komischen ist, was eine Kultur als System bedroht: einerseits der Rückfall in Natur, andererseits die Abgeschnittenheit der Kultur von Natur, ihre unvermittelte Absolutsetzung."[1] Erzgräber attempts to test the validity of Stierle's thesis by applying it initially to the three love visions and then to the *Troilus* and the *Canterbury Tales*. In regard to the four works preceding the *Canterbury Tales*, Erzgräber suggests replacing Stierle's term "bedroht" ("threatens") with "questions", that is, he would modify his statement to read: The object of comicality is anything that questions a culture as system, i.e., either the relapse into nature or the isolation of a culture from nature, that is, a culture presented as an absolute. For the *Canterbury Tales*, however, Erzgräber accepts the validity of Stierle's dictum, while adding that

---

1. K. Stierle, "Komik der Handlung, Komik der Sprachhandlung, Komik der Komödie", in W. Preisendanz und R. Warning (eds.), *Das Komische* (Munich, 1976), p. 260.

in both cases the threat or questioning must be placed in its appropriate historical context. Living in a time of changing cultural values, Chaucer, so Erzgräber maintains, reacted to the interplay of these values and systems by using the instrument of narrative comedy. Comedy, thus, functions as a device to alert his audience to the complexity of their age and to make them conscious of the multifariousness of human nature.

A more historical approach to comedy is taken by Derek Pearsall who prefaces his discussion of "Versions of Comedy in Chaucer's *Canterbury Tales*" by illustrating the breadth of meaning this term carried even for medieval man. Thus, in approaching Chaucer's comic tales, we would be ill advised to take recourse to the classical definition of comedy, also cherished by medieval theorists, as a socially and morally normative form working through the ridicule of vice and folly to the correction of deviancy. The fabliaux, and this is what we generally mean when speaking of Chaucer's comic narratives, set all this aside and illustrate that there are no values, secular or religious, more important than survival and the satisfaction of appetite. As Pearsall says, the fabliaux are a kind of "guerilla warfare on established values". Men here will behave like animals, that is, they are portrayed as slightly less than human. And as such, the view of man in the Chaucerian comic tale is contrasted to that of Chaucerian romance which asserts that man may behave in a noble and self-transcending manner. Both genres are non realistic, one portraying man as subhuman and the other as superhuman; and both are complementary, depicting man according to the respective norms of their genre.

Derek Pearsall's paper and my own are also complementary because both of us stress the concept of genre markers as influencing audience reception. While Pearsall takes an inductive approach, that is, he constitutes the form and meaning of Chaucer's comic tale by selecting from the six fabliaux features they have in common, I take an inductive approach first and then a deductive one. After a survey of the mass of single works called *fabliaux propre ment dits*, I set up a class characterized by a certain group of invariant elements. These invariant elements functioning as genre markers are grouped into four categories: communicative situation, provence of meaning, authorial intent and audience reception. Once this catalogue of characteristic features is established, I compare Chaucer's treatment of the fabliau in the *Shipman's Tale* with the hypothetical model, then I identify the differences, and, finally, I analyse the implications.

The fourth paper dealing with Chaucer's comic tales takes still another approach to this subject. Derek Brewer, analysing the *Reeve's Tale*, places the narrative in the wider context of traditional literature. By this Brewer means a literature showing features characteristic of oral literature even though it is written: The story's identity is fluid; there are many versions and variants; the action is more patterned, and, therefore, more fundamental than the characters; suspense is less important than fulfillment; and the tale has a certain independence of the teller. Since a traditional story has many variations, Brewer stresses the importance of identifying the nucleus which makes the story in question that story and not another one. Applied to the *Reeve's Tale*, Brewer feels that the pattern of the story shows the victory of the young over the old, a victory accompanied by sexual aggression by the young men. As such, the story implies no concern with justice, decency, honesty or other moral values. Since Chaucer, however, places the story within a larger framework and takes pains to make the victim a morally responsible character, he creates a structure of reason and morality not present in other versions of the tale. Brewer describes this process of adaptation as follows: Chaucer took a traditional International Comic Tale, placed it in a dramatic situation, connected the actions, reorientated and deepened the moral implications of the structure, gave it a social dimension, created characters to fit the actions, and enriched the style of the actual narrative. All this is done in the service of social and moral comedy based on the simple but profound observation that "pride goes before a fall", and the biter may be bit.

The transition from the *Reeve's Tale* to "Mary and Love in Fourteenth Century Poetry", the subtitle of Piero Boitani's paper on Marian invocations, may seem daring, yet the presence of such poetry within the *Canterbury Tales* demonstrates that Chaucer conceived of man as a complex being, enveloped in the gross physicality of the senses and yearning for metaphysical purity of the spirit. With bold strokes Boitani sketches the landscape of 14th century Marian prayer, starting appropriately with St. Bernard's invocation of the Virgin in Canto XXXIII of *Paradiso*. He then turns his attention to Guillaume de Deguileville's *Pelecinage de la vie Humaine* and Petrarch's *Canzoniere*. And last, he considers Chaucer's adaptation of these sources in the *ABC*, the *Troilus*, *The Prioress's Tale*, and *The Second Nun's Tale*. His study of the forms and functions of the invocation to Mary illustrates not only fundamental changes in genre and style but also in approaches to religion. We move from narrative to lyric and back to narrative; from fiction to autobiography to allegory and back to fiction; from the figural and austere to a more personal and intimate and finally back to an elevated and controlled style; and from supplication to invocation in the crisis of human life, to private prayer, to celebration and rejection of human love and to the formal prayer prefacing a miracle story first and then a saint's life.

10

The final paper, "The Story-Teller and His Audience – *The Legend of Good Women*", by Dieter Mehl is also concerned with Chaucer's adaptation of source material. The problem of the "right" use of literature is one of the key issues raised in the prologue to this collection of tales in the discussion between the God of Love and the hapless poet so severely criticised by him for his lack of discretion. A rather rigid view of the function of literature is proposed by the god which becomes the aesthetic basis from which the persona has to operate in his recreation of the Ovidian *Heroides*. Dieter Mehl traces this process of adaptation, focusing on the reductions made by a narrator who ostensibly works within the limited framework of his assigned task and thus unwittingly exposes the stories told by him to multifarious readings and judgments. On a higher level than at first apparent, therefore, the issue of transmission, that is, the "right" use of literature, is taken up again, because to believe in old books does not mean mere copying and blind faith but, as Mehl states, critical debate and individual reflection.

It is customary to express one's gratitude at the end of introductions to books and collections of essays. I, too, shall gladly observe this custom because without the generous financial assistance provided by the Friends of the University no lecture series would have been possible and consequently no book. My special thanks also goes to the President of the University, Adolf Theis, who has always shown his appreciation of such esoteric areas of scholarly interest as medieval studies by his unflagging and cheerful support of our various enterprises. And last but certainly not least I would like to thank the contributors for their willingness to participate. I hope that their visit to Tübingen in the spring or early summer carried its own reward.

Tübingen, November 1985   Joerg O. Fichte

The Origins of Comicality in Chaucer

Willi Erzgräber

I

In his article "Comicality of action, comicality of the speech act, comicality of comedy" Karlheinz Stierle makes the following statement:

> The object of comicality is anything that threatens a culture as a system: that is to say, on the one hand the relapse into nature, and on the other hand the isolation of a culture from nature, i.e., its presentation as something absolute.[1]

This thesis shall be tested here on the basis of examples taken from Chaucer's poetry. From his literary beginnings, Chaucer already had an affinity to comicality as a literary form of representation and as a mode of evaluating experience.[2] This can be seen in his first poem, *The Book of the Duchess*, a consolation addressed to his patron John of Gaunt after the death of his wife, Duchess Blanche of Lancaster. The humour with which Chaucer characterizes himself as narrator and dreamer, and the subtle irony with which he meets the Black Knight, shows that he was able to handle the death theme so as to convey to his patron and to a courtly audience a sense of the superiority of man over physical necessity. With reference to Stierle, one could classify excessive mourning as a "relapse into nature", as a breach of courtly decorum. However, if one gives heed to the judgement which Chaucer suggests to his late medieval audience in the comments he has intertwined with the narrative,

---

1. K. Stierle, "Komik der Handlung, Komik der Sprachhandlung, Komik der Komödie", in W. Preisendanz and R. Warning (eds.), *Das Komische* (Munich, 1976), p. 260: "Gegenstand des Komischen ist, was eine Kultur als System bedroht: einerseits der Rückfall in Natur, andererseits die Abgeschnittenheit der Kultur von Natur, ihre unvermittelte Absolutsetzung."
2. See also W. Clemen, *Chaucers frühe Dichtung* (Göttingen, 1963), p.49: "Es ist jedoch kennzeichnend für den Geist des ganzen Gedichtes, daß die trauervolle Ceyx-Halcyone-Episode aufgehellt wird durch einige komische und drastische Einzelheiten, die Chaucer bei Ovid kaum vorgebildet fand."

12

one must arrive at a different conclusion.[3] In Chaucer's view the concentration on death apparent in the monologue of the Black Knight has to be understood as a breach of "lex naturalis", a natural ethical norm which not only demands that man should do good and avoid evil but also admonishes him to preserve his life.[4] Chaucer advocates this very law by means of his irony and comedy.

The element of comicality gains momentum in Chaucer's second poem, *The House of Fame*. Again, the dreamer-narrator is conspicuous in the comical passages. Here, he converses with an eagle sent by Jupiter. During his flight to the House of Fame, the bird gives him a slightly popularized lecture on science, specifically on the nature of sound-waves, thereby kindly widening the narrator's mental horizon. The eagle tells Geoffrey off — backed up by Jupiter's criticism — for burying himself in his books. To put it in Stierle's terminology: in his ironical attacks the bird criticizes "culture being isolated from nature". Jupiter reproaches the narrator, as the eagle reports it:

> . . . ; that thou hast no tydynges
> Of Loves folk yf they be glade,
> Ne of noght elles that God made; (*HF*, 644–646)

The lecturing eagle sets up experience as a contrast to the narrow-mindedness of Geoffrey:

> I preve hyt thus . . .
> Be experience . . . (*HF*, 787-88)

But he can also treat himself with irony, as when he leaves Geoffrey the choice to take his lecture seriously or to smile at it: "Take yt in ernest or in game" (*HF*, 822). Finally, it cannot be ignored that Chaucer the author takes a distanced point of view and makes the irony work against the eagle as well, since the bird who insists so markedly on experience uses as examples of this experience learned sources, such as Plato, Aristotle and probably also Boethius. One thing becomes apparent already at this point: Chaucer does not advocate *one* single standard, but plays with various perspectives and with their rapid interchange surprises a reader who wants to settle down comfortably with one perspective. As author, Chaucer not only plays with the themes which he presents but also with the audience to which his poetry is addressed.

---

3. See e.g. *The Book of the Duchess*, 11. 16–21; all quotations and line numberings refer to *The Works of Geoffrey Chaucer*, ed. F.N. Robinson, 2nd ed. (London, 1957).
4. See Thomas Aquinas, *Summa theologiae*, I–II, q. 94 a. 1–6.

Chaucer mastered the art of changing perspectives in a most subtle way in the third of his early works, *The Parliament of Fowls*.[5] In this poem he combines the popular medieval bird parliament with another popular genre, the dream vision, and tells the story of three eagles wooing a female eagle on the 14th of February, St. Valentine's day, which is, according to popular belief, the traditional day of bird mating. Chaucer distinguishes four different groups of birds: 1) birds of prey, 2) birds that feed on worms and insects, 3) water fowl and 4) birds that feed on seeds. In this hierarchy, and in the way the birds speak and debate, Chaucer criticism has identified an allusion to the English Parliament which was coming into existence at the time. But what is more important than any possible comic-satiric attacks which a contemporary audience might have perceived is the fundamental conflict underlying the debate of the birds, a conflict which resolves around the traditional form of courtly wooing represented by the three eagles' competition for the female eagle. The goose, the duck, and the cuckoo who criticize the courtly lovers confess to their definitely pragmatic attitude. They voice "common sense"; they argue in the same way as Chaucer might hear a man arguing in the streets of London or a merchant at the harbour. The debate reveals the conflict between the social "classes", nobility and bourgeoisie. Both classes are also characterized as representatives of different attitudes towards reality; the rarified idealism of the aristocracy is juxtaposed to the sober realism of the bourgeoisie.

Thus, the question arises whether we have to regard each of these conceptions of reality in Stierle's sense as a cultural system, in such a way that a threat to either one of them has to be regarded as comical, or whether the courtly view of reality must be seen as the norm. In the second case, utterances of the goose, duck and cuckoo would have to be regarded as a "relapse into nature", and these birds would prepare their own comical defeat by their provocation and breach of the aristocratic norm. In order to be able to solve this problem we must take a closer look at some passages of the text.

The royal eagle who speaks first proves to be a worthy representative of nobility in manner, gestures, choice of words and argument. His address to the female eagle is an immaculate declaration of courtly love:

> "Unto my soverayn lady, and not my fere,
> I chese, and chese with wil, and herte, and thought,
> The formel on youre hond, so wel iwrought,

---

5. See also W. Clemen's comment on "die 'doppelte Sicht'" as a dramatic device in Chaucer's *Parliament of Fowls*, in *Chaucers frühe Dichtung*, p. 205 ff.

> Whos I am al, and evere wol hire serve,
> Do what hire lest, to do me lyve or sterve;
>
> "Besekynge hire of merci and of grace,
> As she that is my lady sovereyne;
> Or let me deye present in this place.
> For certes, longe may I nat lyve in payne,
> For in myn herte is korven every veyne.
> Havynge reward only to my trouthe,
> My deere herte, have on my wo som routhe.
>
> "And if that I to hyre be founde untrewe,
> Disobeysaunt, or wilful necligent,
> Avauntour, or in proces love a newe,
> I preye to yow this be my jugement,
> That with these foules I be al torent,
> That ilke day that evere she me fynde
> To hir untrewe, or in my gilt unkynde.
>
> "And syn that non loveth hire so wel as I,
> Al be she nevere of love me behette,
> Thanne oughte she be myn thourgh hire mercy,
> For other bond can I non on hire knette.
> Ne nevere for no wo ne shal I lette
> To serven hire, how fer so that she wende;
> Say what yow list, my tale is at an ende."
>
> (*PF*, 416—441)

Distinction, solemn pathos and elegance characterize the careful language of the royal eagle. The two other suitors are of lower birth, "of lower kynde", and this is noticeable in their use of language.[6] When the second eagle states in his speech

> "I dar ek seyn, if she me fynde fals,
> Unkynde, janglere, or rebel any wyse,
> Or jelous, do me hangen by the hals!
>
> (*PF*, 456—458)

his language is, admittedly, more expressive and richer in imagery; it is, however, of a lower standard compared to the diction of the royal eagle, and, in contrast, it even has a slightly comical effect.

---

6. See also D. Mehl's interpretation in *Geoffrey Chaucer. Eine Einführung in seine erzählenden Dichtungen* (Berlin, 1973), pp. 62—64.

Yet the comical impact is much stronger when the goose, cuckoo and duck chip in with their objections. The narrator puts it thus:

> The goos, the cokkow, and the doke also
> So cryede, "Kek kek! kokkow! quek quek!" hye,
> That thorugh myne eres the noyse wente tho.
> The goos seyde, "Al this nys not worth a flye!

(*PF*, 498–501)

The primitive language as an inroad into the territory of a courtly "culture as system" seems – at first glance – ridiculous. This effect is emphasized above all by the fact that the nobility can talk at length, but their adversaries are only allowed brief remarks. The balance changes when the goddess of nature suggests that all four groups choose a speaker who is to judge the three eagles' courtship. The advocates of a chivalrous way of life and courtly love are the falcon (for the birds of prey), the sparrow-hawk, the turtle dove and two more falcons; they are opposed by the goose, duck and cuckoo. In this debate, which does not decide the issue in favour of one of the parties concerned, the representatives of common sense become more convincing. The conventions of chivalry seem to be at cross purposes with reality. They seem to force an impractical and unnatural behaviour on the eagles; the speeches in defence of the ideal of service in courtly love seem to support the thesis of the isolation of a "culture from nature". Thus Chaucer emphasizes the ironic-satiric effect of the attacks launched by the lower birds.

The decision made by the goddess of nature gives a clue to the way in which Chaucer wanted the reader to understand the basic conflict of the poem: each of the birds, with the exception of the three eagles, receives a mate. The eagles have to serve for another year – this is what nature asks them to do in compliance with the female eagle's request. During this year they can prove their worthiness. From this decision we can conclude that Chaucer – from a superior vantage-point – recognizes the value and the limitations of both ways of life, the "middle-class" pragmatic one of the lower birds and the idealistic-chivalrous one of the eagles. Each has its justification as well as its necessary limitations which become obvious in the juxtaposition with the other "class" and which are presented in a comic light in the dialogue. But we can also see clearly that the narrator's manipulation of the reader's sympathy – the words and behaviour of the goddess of nature are the most effective means of this manipulation – still reveals a medieval hierarchy in which the courtly way of life is superior to the pragmatic one of the bourgeoisie. If there is a superior system in this poem into which both the nobility and the bourgeoisie can be fitted, then the goddess of nature is the represent-ative of this system. She accepts and encourages the creature's biological drive to procreate as well as the forms of civilization and refinements of human communal life. Chaucer's concept of nature – and this *The Parlia-ment of Fowls* proves clearly – is shaped by the medieval concept of "lex naturae" or "lex naturalis". In this context I refer to Thomas Aquinas, *Summa Theologiae*, I–II, q. 94, a passage in which Thomas says that the law of nature comprises "the union of male and female, the rearing of off-spring and the like" as well as any inclination of man towards the good in accordance with his reason, which means his natural inclination to acquire knowledge of God and to live in a community.[7]

II

That Chaucer was strongly influenced by these concepts can be seen very clearly when we look at his adaptation and narrative re-creation of Boccac-cio's *Il Filostrato*, an epic poem which he called *Troilus and Criseyde*.[8] In this work he developed and refined the technique of comic characterization of protagonists which he had already used in *The Parliament of Fowls*.

Troilus is introduced as a young knight who mocks all those who render ser-vice in love, and the narrator inserts the following comment:

> Forthy ensample taketh of this man,
> Ye wise, proude, and worthi folkes alle,
> To scornen Love, which that so soone kan
> The fredom of youre hertes to hym thralle;
> For evere it was, and evere it shal byfalle,
> That Love is he that alle thing may bynde,
> For may no man fordon the lawe of kynde.

(*TC*, I, 232–238)

---

7. See Thomas Aquinas, *Summa theologiae*, I–II, q. 94 a. 2: Et secundum hoc, dicun-tur ea esse de lege naturali quae natura omnia animalia docuit, ut est coniunctio maris et feminae, et educatio liberorum, et similia.
Tertio modo inest homini inclinatio ad bonum secundum naturam rationis, quae est sibi propria, sicut homo habet naturalem inclinationem ad hoc quod veritatem cog-noscat de deo, et ad hoc quod in societate vivat.
8. For a detailed interpretation of the tragic and comic elements in Chaucer's *Troilus and Criseyde* see my essay "Tragik und Komik in Chaucers 'Troilus and Criseyde'", in W. Erzgräber (ed.), *Geoffrey Chaucer* (Darmstadt, 1983), pp. 144–175.

The narrator refers explicitly to the law of nature which is common to all human beings and from which, in the narrator's opinion, nobody ought to exempt himself. Those who think they can do so are "blind" and "proud" in the judgement of the narrator. In his blind arrogance, Troilus seems a comic figure. He changes as soon as he sets eyes on Criseyde and experiences for the first time what it means to love another person.

The description of his behaviour in books I, II and III corresponds in all its details to the code of courtly love: Troilus experiences love as a sickness, is silent about it, mourns and laments when he can see no possibility to confess his love to Criseyde, and refuses to tell his love's name when Pandarus asks him for the reason of his suffering. But the diplomatic and clever Pandarus is well-versed in rhetoric. He succeeds in learning Troilus' long-kept secret and he persuades him to follow all his (Pandarus') advice. The inner perfection which Troilus reaches through his love of Criseyde is summarized by the narrator at the end of book III in the following comment:

> And though that he be come of blood roial,
> Hym liste of pride at no wight for to chace;
> Benigne he was to ech in general,
> For which he gat hym thank in every place.
> Thus wolde Love, yheried be his grace,
> That Pride, Envye, and Ire, and Avarice
> He gan to fle, and everich other vice.

> (*TC*, III, 1800–1806)

The song of praise to love as a cosmic power which Chaucer gave Troilus to sing in the same context and which he modelled on Boethius' *Consolatio Philosophiae* proves that Troilus understood the system of the world through his experience and his reason, a system to which he was subjected from the beginning, as the narrator explains. We must emphasize, however, that Troilus is a comic figure all the way through his inner change which Chaucer describes in the first three books. In his conception of love, Troilus undoubtedly follows the courtly system. But he is always too weak to achieve alone the goal which he sets himself in his thoughts, hopes and wishes, his dreams and illusions. This can be interpreted as an individual trait in Troilus' character; but when the epic is seen in its literary and cultural context, one cannot ignore the fact that the ideal of chivalry which Troilus represents paradigmatically had passed its prime in the 80s of the 14th century. We only have to remember that Chrétien de Troyes wrote in the second half of the 12th century and that the Middle High German epics date from the beginning of the 13th century. In Chaucer's time courtly poetry, and particularly the idea of service

18

in courtly love, had already acquired an element of romanticism.[9] In Troilus, Chaucer illustrates a way of life which was no longer as binding for the society of his time as it had probably been for the society in which the German and French courtly epics had been composed. In this way, Chaucer was able to sketch the outlines of a courtly ideal (which, moreover, he transferred in this work into antiquity) and, at the same time, to point out the limitations of this ideal.

To the degree in which Troilus relies on Pandarus – a friend who refuses to be looked upon as a bawd – he is subjected to the law of "Fremdbestimmtheit",[10] i.e. to being governed extraneously. According to recent investigations of comicality, this situation is a prerequisite for the provocation of laughter in the reader who is amused by a lover with these highflown ideals.

The best example for "extraneous government" influencing Troilus is the scene in book III, in which the reader learns about all the clever tricks which Pandarus uses to bring Troilus and Criseyde together. When Troilus has finally made it to Criseyde's bedside, he faints: "And down he fel al sodeynly a-swowne" (*TC*, III, 1092). Again, Pandarus' 'grasp' is necessary to unite the lovers:

> ... !" but certeyn, at the laste,
> For this or that, he into bed hym caste,
> And seyde, "O thef, is this a mannes herte?"
> And of he rente al to his bare sherte;
>
> And seyde, "Nece, but ye helpe us now,
> Allas, youre owen Troilus is lorn!"
> "Iwis, so wolde I, and I wiste how,
> Ful fayn," quod she; "Allas, that I was born!"
>
> (*TC*, III, 1096–1103)

In speech and action Pandarus demonstrates the same mentality as was expressed by the duck, goose and cuckoo in *The Parliament of Fowls*. Pandarus, too, comments on Troilus' wooing, his laments and his sadness with witty repartee, in expressive language full of rich imagery, combining proverbs and philosophical maxims with such skill that Troilus can often escape him only

9. For a detailed discussion of this aspect of Chaucer's courtly poetry see U. Schaefer, *Höfisch-ritterliche Dichtung und sozialhistorische Realität. Literatursoziologische Studien zum Verhältnis von Adelsstruktur, Ritterideal und Dichtung bei Geoffrey Chaucer* (Frankfurt/M. & Bern, 1977).
10. K. Stierle, loc. cit., p. 254.

with an angry gesture. In contrast to *The Parliament of Fowls*, this pragmatic mentality is not attributed to a member of a lower class but to a friend of Troilus who has the same social status. Seen in the large context of social development this would mean that Pandarus represents a section of the aristocracy which has already taken over to a large extent modes of thought and ways of life originally belonging to the bourgeoisie. Indeed, this situation has its parallels in English social history, not only in the 14th century, but also later, particularly in the 18th century.

We cannot ignore, however, that even though Troilus and Pandarus belong to the same social class, the confrontation of their concepts of life has its comical effects. Pandarus' comments reveal the limitations and weaknesses of a highly developed chivalrous way of life. On the other hand, Troilus' answers reveal Pandarus' limitations, who in spite of his cleverness and cunning has not succeeded in reaching his goal as courtly lover. When Pandarus begins to give Troilus lessons in the *Ars Amatoria*, Troilus draws his friend's attention to the irony of the latter's situation:

> "Thow koudest nevere in love thiselven wisse:
> How devel maistow brynge me to blisse?"
>
> (*TC*, I, 622–623)

Pandarus' answer shows that he is well aware of his position – in good-humoured irony he calls himself a fool – but he believes that he has enough experience at his command to be able to guide Troilus: "A fool may ek a wis-man ofte gide" (*TC*, I, 630). Thus, Pandarus and Troilus appear as sages and as fools simultaneously who can take part in a love comedy with different roles and functions.

Chaucer explored new ways of comicality in the characterization of Pandarus insofar as he allocated two roles to him: he is the director of a love comedy in which he himself plays the leading part. His subtle directing manifests itself in manœuvering not only Troilus but also Criseyde and the whole circle of friends into roles that fit in with his plot. Through the roles which Pandarus allocates them Troilus and Criseyde are forced to follow their secret wishes which they have tried to suppress in consideration of society. In this drama Pandarus develops into such a dominant figure that the narrator remarks in book II: "But God and Pandare wist al what this mente" (*TC*, II, 1561). Pandarus organizes the love play as a sort of comic predestination, he pulls the strings, arranges situations and on top of that parodies the conventional forms of service in courtly love and its formulas of speech. In book I, for example, he assumes the role of a priest of the god Amor and makes Troilus confess before this god that he is guilty of arrogant and mocking remarks about Amor's servants. Pandarus gives him absolution with the subtle elegance and lightheartedness of the comedian (cf. *TC*, I, 932 ff.).

The role of director strengthens Pandarus' conviction that he can overcome all the obstacles facing the lovers with cunning and plotting and that he can manipulate everyday life completely to his own liking. He is fairly triumphant when he succeeds in figuring out in advance the cosmic-meteorological constellations which are propitious for the lovers' future. Pandarus thus falls victim to an illusion which begins to be destroyed from book IV onwards by the course of events, i.e. by fortune, as well as by Calchas. Although Pandarus keeps talking about Fortune's power, he thinks he can outwit her. In contrast to Boethius who allowed for man's freeing his inner self from fortune only if – metaphorically speaking – he moves towards the centre of the wheel and looks for stability in God (cf. *Consolatio Philosophiae*, IV, 6), Pandarus remains caught in a purely temporal system. He thinks he can settle on the periphery of the wheel by means of cunning and can survive in this manner. He is so blind to the world order that he violates a norm which is fundamental to all cosmic, social and natural events; he even provokes this order when he assumes the role of the director of earthly events. This violation of norms initiates a countermovement which unmasks his cosmic blindness and makes him at least partially a tragic figure. On the whole, that is to say, he becomes a tragicomic character. It is his tragedy that on the one hand he wants to promote the lovers' fortune with all his efforts in a purely unselfish way (and he succeeds in promoting it), but that on the other hand his plans fail because of the exchange of prisoners in accordance with Calchas' wishes and Criseyde's faithlessness. These are events, however, which illustrate in an exemplary way the laws of fortune. In outline form, a type of tragedy emerges here which was to serve Shakespeare again and again as the foundation for dramatic action and which is defined in *Hamlet*: "our thoughts are ours, their ends none of our own" (III, 2).[11] The best intentions of Shakespeare's tragic heroes as well as of Pandarus turn into their contrary once they have become action without the protagonists being able to check the course of this development.

The comic silencing of Pandarus takes place in book V where one reads that he stood still as a stone and was silent, "a word ne kowde he seye" (*TC*, V,

---

11. See W.F. Schirmer, *Geschichte der englischen und amerikanischen Literatur von den Anfängen bis zur Gegenwart* (Tübingen, 1959), I, 266.

1729). When he finally says something, he must admit, ironically, "I kan namore seye" (*TC*, V, 1743). He is silent in sadness about Troilus' fate and in shame about Criseyde's behaviour. When Pandarus, the master of words and rhetoric, speaks again, he can only state that his cunning has failed and that he has come to the end of his resources, even of his verbal art.

In respect to Pandarus I would broaden Stierle's definition slightly and add that the object of comicality in Chaucer is not only that which threatens a culture as a system but also any conscious revolt against the world order outlined in the *Consolatio Philosophiae* that Chaucer considered binding. (We should remind ourselves that Chaucer translated Boethius before he adapted Boccaccio's *Il Filostrato*).

That man's blindness to the system of the world is ridiculed in Chaucer's *Troilus and Criseyde* is proved by the last scene in which laughter can be heard, namely at the end of book V when we hear that Troilus was transferred to the eighth sphere after his death. When he looks down onto the small earth and perceives human beings who mourn his death, he laughs:

> And in hymself he lough right at the wo
> Of hem that wepten for his deth so faste;
> And dampned al oure werk that foloweth so
> The blynde lust, the which that may nat laste,
> And sholden al oure herte on heven caste.
>
> (*TC*, V, 1821–25)

Troilus laughs about humans who lament the transitoriness of all earthly things and whose sadness about the mutability of the temporal blocks their view of the permanence of the eternal. This comicality — which may be surprising to the modern reader — helps to put a reversal of the hierarchical (medieval) world picture into proper perspective.

Troilus and Criseyde shows clearly how two views overlap in Chaucer's work. One is the anthropocentric view, in which the concepts of value cherished by the aristocracy and the bourgeoisie rival each other; the other is the theocentric one, which both medieval philosophy and theology had taught him. Each of these views contains concepts of norms; and the complexity of Chaucer's poetry, as well as its comic effects, arises from the fact that he continuously reflected on the values and limitations of the norms advocated by the aristocracy and the bourgeoisie,[12] and that he tried to define the

---

12. For a discussion of this issue see also C. Muscatine, *Chaucer and the French Tradition. A Study in Style and Meaning* (Berkeley & Los Angeles, 1957), pp. 124–165.

22

merits of all things temporal before the backdrop of the immutable and absolute.

III

In *Troilus and Criseyde* the language and the facial expressions of Troilus and Pandarus represent, as it were, two literary genres which are juxtaposed in a contrapuntal manner, namely romance and fabliau. At the beginning of the *Canterbury Tales* these genres are separate. First the Knight tells about the fates of Palamon and Arcite who court Emily in a romance with philosophical overtones, in which the war-like and the erotic components of chivalry are dramatized. If we believe the narrator who provides a link to the next tale, the romance should have been followed by the Monk's tale. But the drunken Miller pushes himself forward and tells a burlesque, and in some passages even obscene story for which Chaucer apologizes to the audience in a gracious and ironic manner:

> What sholde I moore seyn, but this Millere
> He nolde his wordes for no man forbere,
> But tolde his cherles tale in his manere.
> M'athynketh that I shal reherce it heere.
> And therfore every gentil wight I preye,
> For Goddes love, demeth nat that I seye
> Of yvel entente, but for I moot reherce
> Hir tales alle, be they bettre or werse,
> Or elles falsen som of my mateere.
> And therfore, whoso list it nat yheere,
> Turne over the leef and chese another tale;
>
> (I(A) 3167–77)

Even before the Miller tells his story he announces that it will be about a carpenter who is cuckolded by a student; he thus provokes a harsh reply from the Reeve who is a carpenter by profession and who feels his status has been impaired. A detailed analysis shows, however, that the comedy in the *Miller's Tale*, simple as it may look at first glance, is directed at various quarters.[13] This is due to the context of the story, the characterization of the protagonists and the complex narrative situation. Although the actual teller of the story is the Miller, there is a manipulating author behind him who is superior

---

13. See A. David, *The Strumpet Muse. Art and Morals in Chaucer's Poetry* (Bloomington & London, 1976), pp. 92–97.

to the common and coarse ways of a workman, but who also ridicules – as the parody found in the *Tale of Sir Thopas* shows – certain conventions of the chivalrous narrative situation and exposes them to the mocking laughter of his audience. In addition to that, the audience within the *Canterbury Tales* who listens to the story is composed of various social classes. There is the aristocracy, the clergy, the bourgeoisie, and finally a Plowman who belongs, together with his brother, the Parish Priest, and the Knight, to the positive figures in the *Canterbury Tales*. Knight, Parish Priest and Plowman represent the three estates in the conception of the early and late Middle Ages, and since they are all presented in an idealized way by the author, they can be regarded as representing the norms of their estates. The structure of the audience on the one hand and the co-ordination of the tales and their intende d effects on the other hand contribute to a multiplicity of relations, meanings and effects which were obvious also to the medieval audience which felt itself represented in the pilgrims. The judgement of some stories is unanimous: the pilgrims agree that the Knight's tale is "a noble storie" (I(A) 3111). But their judgement of the comic stories is controversial.

In the *Miller's Tale*, Alison, the wife of John the Carpenter, is courted by two lovers, Absalon and Nicholas, and particularly Absalon uses courtly forms of wooing. Given this view of the plot, we can interpret the fabliau as a parody on the *Knight's Tale* which preceded it, especially since it is based on the same fundamental constellation: a woman is courted by two men in the language appropriate to their status. The chivalry which the Miller presents in the character of Absalon can clearly be seen in the outer appearance of this clerk of the parish of Oxford:

> Now was ther of that chirche a parissh clerk,
> The which that was ycleped Absolon.
> Crul was his heer, and as the gold it shoon,
> And strouted as a fanne large and brode;
> Ful streight and evene lay his joly shode.
> His rode was reed, his eyen greye as goos.
> With Poules wyndow corven on his shoos,
> In hoses rede he wente fetisly.
>
> (I(A) 3312–3319)

He is dressed in fashionable clothes; like the knight's son whom Chaucer portrays in the "General Prologue", he can sing and dance as befits a "young squier":

> In twenty manere koude he trippe and daunce
> After the scole of Oxenforde tho,
> And with his legges casten to and fro,
>
> (I(A) 3328–30)

In characterizing his behaviour and his treatment of women, the narrator uses adjectives and phrases which are typical of the courtly lover of romances. He is called "jolif (. . .) and gay" (I(A) 3339), "jolif and amorous" (I(A) 3355), and when he sings a song to his beloved, he uses the diction and imagery of Solomon's Song of Songs (cf. (I(A) 3698—3706).

If we take into consideration, however, that Absalon is a cleric who acts like a courtly lover, we realize that the comic aspects of his behaviour can be understood as estate satire: he assumes forms of chivalrous behaviour which do not fit his status. "The object of comicality is that which threatens a culture as a system": here the threat of one cultural system (the clerical) to another (the chivalrous) causes a comic "relapse into nature", which happens several times when the narrator speaks of the sensual and even lustful desire of Absalon. Absalon's chivalrous affectations resemble an ill-fitting garment which cannot hide his true nature. The escape from what Stierle calls the "cultural system" is twofold in the case of Absalon. He goes beyond the clerical system to which he belongs by way of his profession, but he also goes beyond the chivalrous system into which he tries to fit but which is not appropriate to him and which he cannot master.

One could regard Absalon as proof of Nykrog's thesis that the fabliaux belong to the sphere of chivalrous poetry in which the knights mock the inadequate imitation of their culture by lower social classes.[14] When we take into account that Chaucer presented the tale to a predominantly courtly audience, such an interpretation of Absalon seems convincing. The comedy to which he falls victim demands a subtle understanding between Chaucer the author and his courtly audience. The irony of the passages in which Absalon apes courtly behaviour — and Alison admits that she wants to make a fool of him — could be compared to the ironic wink which might have accompanied Chaucer's presentation and have given a clue to his artistic intentions. The coarse disillusionment which Absalon experiences in his role as lover — Alison turns round quickly at the window in the middle of a pitch-dark night when he wants to kiss her so that he does not meet her mouth but her backside — this disillusionment not only destroys his hopes as lover but also exposes to ridicule his courtly affectations.

But it should not be forgotten that the teller of the tale, the Miller, is a member of the lower social classes so that one cannot completely refute the older

14. See P. Nykrog, Les Fabliaux. Etude d'histoire littéraire et de stylistique médiévale (Copenhagen, 1957).

thesis, formulated by Joseph Bédier, which held that the fabliaux were coarse "contes à rire" told by the bourgeoisie to the bourgeoisie in order to express its protest against hybrid forms of chivalrous culture by describing unbridled sensuality.[15] The representative of the bourgeois morality would be Alison, with all her sensuality, who spends the night with the student Nicholas.[16] If we analyse Alison's characterization given at the beginning of the tale, we can see that she is to be regarded as the embodiment of youth and life spilling over with joyful and pleasurable vitality, even as nature itself which rebels against all constraints and restrictions. The images and comparisons which are used to describe Alison express this clearly. They are taken from the sphere of animal and vegetable creation and give a clue to the interpretation of Alison's outer appearance and behaviour. She is not to be judged according to any social or moral norms. Here are a few quotations taken from Alison's elaborate description to prove this point:

> Ful smale ypulled were hire browes two,
> And tho were bent and blake as any sloo.
> She was ful moore blisful on to see
> Than is the newe pere-jonette tree,
> And softer than the wolle is of a wether.
> . . .
> Ful brighter was the shynyng of hir hewe
> Than in the Tour the noble yforged newe.
> But of hir song, it was as loude and yerne
> As any swalwe sittynge on a berne.
> Therto she koude skippe and make game,
> As any kyde or calf folwynge his dame.
> Hir mouth was sweete as bragot or the meeth,
> Or hoord of apples leyd in hey or heeth.
> Wynsynge she was, as is a joly colt,
> Long as a mast, and upright as a bolt.

(I(A) 3245–49; 3255–64)

Alison is never shown in any comic light or subjected to any punishment in the sense of "poetic justice", and this is another factor which strengthens the view that Chaucer in his role as author and narrator looks at his protagonist with sympathy. She survives all turbulences of the nocturnal comedy of errors

---

15. J. Bédier, *Les Fabliaux*, 5th ed. (Paris, 1925). – For a discussion of Bédier's and Nykrog's theories see D.S. Brewer, "The Fabliaux", in B. Rowland, ed., *Companion to Chaucer Studies* (Toronto, New York, London, 1968), pp. 247 ff.
16. For further comments on Alison see A. David, *The Strumpet Muse*, pp. 96–97.

without physical damage and without loss of social prestige. The comedy in the love game is directed on the one hand — as shown above — against foolish Absalon, who is made fun of by Alison and her lover and who is blind enough to think that he can cuckold the old carpenter.

On the other hand, the comedy is directed against Nicholas, the gloating student, who wants to intensify his triumph over his rival and wants to make a fool of him in the same way as Alison had done. But poetic justice is rather crude; it is branded into his backside with a red-hot iron.

A comic poetic justice is finally visited on the jealous and superstitious carpenter. He believes in Nicholas' cock-and-bull story which predicts a second flood — Nicholas pretends to have perceived this in his astrological studies.

The carpenter is easily talked into making three wooden tubs in which he wants to survive the disaster together with Alison and Nicholas. So he falls blindly into the trap set for him by the young lovers. He turns out to be the husband who has watched over his wife like a prison guard but is nevertheless outwitted by her. At the end of the story it is he who is the laughing-stock of all his neighbours:

> The folk gan laughen at his fantasye;
> Into the roof they kiken and they cape,
> And turned al his harm unto a jape.
> For what so that this carpenter answerde,
> It was for noght, no man his reson herde.
> With othes grete he was so sworn adoun
> That he was holde wood in al the toun;
> For every clerk anonright heeld with oother.
> They seyde, "The man is wood, my leeve brother";
> And every wight gan laughen at this stryf.
>
> (I(A) 3840—49)

IV

If we measure Chaucer's works interpreted so far against Stierle's definition of comicality, it becomes necessary to change one of his critical terms. If we take into account the interplay between the culture of the aristocracy and that of the bourgeoisie which Chaucer demonstrates as masterly as the contract he draws between them, and if we agree from a theological or philosophical point of view, Stierle's dictum "the object of comicality is that which *threatens* a culture as a system" would have to be changed to the phrase "the object of comicality is that which *questions* a culture as a system". However, if we look at the *Canterbury Tales*, we can see that Stierle's definition is justified for Chaucer's last major work.

The character who attacks clerical culture most decisively, in triumphant vitalistic gestures as well as with an ingenious rhetoric taken from humanist and clerical traditions, and who subjects this culture most ruthlessly to laughter is the Wife of Bath. Her prologue is one of the artistic highlights of the *Canterbury Tales.*[17]

This prologue is a "threat" − in Stierle's sense − to the cultural system of medieval theology and philosophy insofar as it parodies the methods of "argumentatio" and "disputatio" which were developed by the clergy, in order literally to pervert traditional concepts of the man-woman relationship and, moreover, the conventional hierarchy of material and spiritual values. It is typical of the Wife of Bath's treatment of authorities that she refers to a wealth of quotations, from Jesus, Solomon and St. Paul to Socrates, Ovid and Theophrastus, in order to prove her theses. But she has recourse to a number of stratagems, which are included under the term "glosing", in order to change and interpret her quotations so that they conform to her preconceived ideas. She does not hesitate to quote only parts of a phrase, re-interpreting the fragments to suit her meaning, nor to ignore the context of her quotations.

She certainly knows the theological doctrine of the hierarchy of ways of life open to women, with virginity at the top and widowhood and marriage as the two lower levels, and she is quite ready to accept the high valuation of the ideal of virginity. But she argues skilfully in order to present her opinion which deviates from the traditional view. She refers − like a preacher − to the second epistle to Tim. 2, 20, which says: "In a great house there are not only vessels of gold and silver but also of wood and earthenware, and some for noble use, some for ignoble." She speaks up for the wooden vessels (i.e. the wives), because they fulfill a purpose, and devaluates the golden vessels (the virgins), because they do not. She also quotes St. Paul as her witness for the fact that virginity is only recommended, not commanded:

---

17. For my comments on *The Wife of Bath's Prologue* I am also indebted to D.R. Howard, *The Idea of the Canterbury Tales* (Berkeley, Los Angeles, London, 1976), pp. 247−255; A. David, *The Strumpet Muse*, pp. 135−153; D. Aers, *Chaucer, Langland and the Creative Imagination* (London, Boston, Henley, 1980), pp. 146−152 and pp. 156−157. See also my essay on "'Auctoritee' and 'Experience' in Chaucer", in Piero Boitani and Anna Torti (eds.), *Intellectuals and Writers in Fourteenth-Century Europe* (Tübingen, 1985), pp. 67−87.

Th'apostel, whan he speketh of maydenhede,
He seyde that precept therof hadde he noon.
Men may conseille a womman to been oon,
But conseillyng is no comandement.

(III (D) 64—67)

It is typical of the Wife of Bath's clever and artful way of arguing her point that she adds expressive imagery to support her argument:

And certes, if ther were no seed ysowe,
Virginitee, thanne wherof sholde it growe?

(III (D) 71—72)

Here she tries to outwit the clergy by means of common sense. Her strategy aims at redeeming marriage from its inferior position and granting it priority, because it is the necessary basis of the continuity of mankind. She refers to the Old Testament, Gen 1, 28: "be fruitful and multiply" but also to the New Testament, Matth. 19,5: "For this reason a man shall leave his father and mother and be joined to his wife, and the two shall become one."

Her interpretation of biblical authorities leads her to the conclusion that second and third marriages are not forbidden anywhere. Here, she contradicts current medieval ecclesiastical law but not common practice, as every Englishman could observe in his neighbourhood among aristocratic families. The passages which clerics quoted in her time for only one marriage, namely the wedding at Cana and Christ's meeting with the Samaritan woman, she invalidates by reference to the 1st epistle to the Corinthians 7, 39, which says: "A wife is bound to her husband as long as he lives. If the husband dies, she is free to be married to whom she wishes, only in the Lord."

Finally, she opposes the view that sexuality in marriage only serves to beget children. She stands up eloquently for sensual enjoyment of sexuality and says: "(. . .) I koude noght withdrawe /My chambre of Venus from a good felawe" (III (D) 617—618). These and similar passages in the prologue prove that the Wife of Bath opposes the verdict against sensuality and sex which was very common, particularly in early medieval theology (influenced by St. Augustine). She also turns against all anti-feminist doctrines as they can be found in an anthology which her fifth husband studies with pleasure. The authors represented in this anthology are, among others, Jerome, *Epistola Adversus Jovinianum*, (a treatise often used by Chaucer); Theophrastus, *Liber de Nuptiis*; Walter Map, *Epistola Valerii ad Rufinum de non Ducenda Uxore*.[18] The

---

18. See *The Works of Geoffrey Chaucer*, ed. F.N. Robinson, p. 701.

marital disputes which the Wife of Bath carries out with Jenkin, her fifth husband, reach their climax when she tears three pages out of this anthology and forces him – after he has taken his revenge on her with brute force – to burn the book. Here, the Wife of Bath's monologue turns into a small dramatized marriage comedy, a farce like those which the audience could have watched between Noah and his wife on the stage in the mystery plays.

According to the Wife of Bath's statement, her experience with her five husbands itself suffices for her to express a valid view on marriage:

> "Experience, though noon auctoritee
> Were in this world, is right ynogh for me
> To speke of wo that is in mariage;
>
> (III (D) 1–3)

Her autobiographical reports, but also her comments and the advice which she wants to give other wives, and which she thinks is justified on the basis of her variegated experience, are more than the mere corroboration of the things the authorities say about the "yoke of mariage". Her arguments aim at putting traditional doctrine in a comic light. The satirical strategy, well-founded in psychology, which the Wife of Bath employs when she refutes the arguments quoted from authorities is most probably due to suggestions taken up from the second part of the *Roman de la Rose*.[19] Like Jean de Meung the Wife of Bath claims that anti-feminist views and judgements are no more than the twaddle of old men, whose lack of vitality prevents them from serving the goddess Venus:

> The clerk, whan he is oold, and may noght do
> Of Venus werkes worth his olde sho,
> Thanne sit he doun, and writ in his dotage
> That wommen kan nat kepe hir mariage!
>
> (III (D) 707–710)

It would be wrong, however, to characterize the Wife of Bath as nothing but the ironic-satiric critic of orthodox tradition. Progressive as her ideas may seem when she fights against the contempt of women and sexuality, she remains within the boundaries of the medieval concept of a male-dominated society when talking about the aims she sets for herself in her marriages. She

---

19. See D.M. Murtaugh, "Women in Geoffrey Chaucer", *ELH*, 38 (1971), 473–92; repr. in W. Erzgräber (ed.), *Geoffrey Chaucer*, pp. 336–365.

strives for a change in the paradigm of male-female relations only insofar as she wants to replace male dominance by female dominance. Her prologue and tale both culminate in the demand that "maistrie" and "soveraynetee" are the woman's due. At the end of her account of her fifth marriage, in which she succeeds in taming an anti-feminist man who is a clerk to boot, we find the following verses:

> He yaf me al the bridel in myn hond,
> To han the governance of hous and lond,
> And of his tonge, and of his hond also;
> And made hym brenne his book anon right tho.
> And whan that I hadde geten unto me,
> By maistrie, al the soveraynetee,
> And that he seyde, 'Myn owene trewe wyf,
> Do as thee lust the terme of al thy lyf;
> Keep thyn honour, and keep eek myn estaat' –
>
> (III (D) 813–821)

Medieval theology in accordance with St. Paul taught that women ought to be subject to their husbands and that the man is the woman's head; with her subtle and ironic rhetoric the Wife of Bath aims for the contrary: she pleads for the woman's mastery over the man. But this mastery not only refers to physical relations, it also means sovereignty on the economic level. In the Middle Ages marriage was widely considered to be a business arrangement in which the woman lost all claims to personal property. The Wife of Bath, however, wants to draw a business advantage from love and marriage. She is well aware of the 'market value'[20] – as an American critic puts it – of her body; she wants to acquire property through marriage and, finally, she wants to control this property unchecked and follow her amorous inclinations in freedom. In spite of her criticism of everyday life in marriage, she does not change anything in the fundamental structures of dominance as they are mirrored in the behaviour of the men she attacks or in the literary satires she mocks. She only reverses the premises from male to female. As much as the Wife of Bath seems to triumph over all authorities in her exuberant self-portrait, to the same degree she remains tied to traditional concepts in her protest. Her conscious attacks on husbands and clerks contribute to the involuntary unmasking of her conventional mentality; thus, she becomes the victim of an ingeniously constructed piece of dramatic irony on Chaucer's part. She objects to the "isolation from nature" which she perceives in clerical as well as

---

20. A. David, *The Strumpet Muse*, p. 146.

31

in humanist critics of the female sex, but she gets herself into a tight spot. She claims to set free female nature, but she sets up a system of dominance which only *seems* to be new. Chaucer dissociates himself with authorial irony.

V

That Chaucer considered these tensions between theological and philosophical authorities on the one hand and the rebellious vitality directed against them on the other hand as a constant source of comic conflicts is evident above all in the portraits of the clergy which are included in the prologue of the *Canterbury Tales*. In the narrative development of these conflicts in the introductory portraits, we can perceive a subtle refinement of presentation at the point where Chaucer "internalized" the conflicts.[21] While the opposing forces in the Wife of Bath's self-portrait – for example the fifth husband as its representative of a traditional cultural system and she as the critical and satiric assailant – face each other like the antagonists in a drama, the conflict between systems of culture and values in the prologue to the *Canterbury Tales* takes place within the characters.

Let us take the portrait of the Monk as an example (I (A), 165–207). His life ought to be subjected to the Benedictine rule of "ora et labora" to which Chaucer refers in the phrase "The reule of seint Maure or of seint Beneit" (173). The Monk, however, follows the inclinations of his nature: he enjoys eating a fat swan ("A fat swan loved he best of any roost", 206), he dresses like an elegant nobleman ("I seigh his sleves purfiled at the hond / With grys, and that the fyneste of a lond", 193–194) and his outer appearance evokes the impression of an epicure who sates himself on the sensual joys of life ("He was a lord ful fat and in good poynt", 200).

With reference to Stierle's definition which we took as a starting point for our analysis of comicality in Chaucer we could say that the monk disturbs the "isolation of spiritual culture from nature" in the Benedictine rule; "(. . .) it was old and somdel streit" (174), so that he feels called upon to balance this defect in an almost naive and joyful way.

---

21. The term "internalize" goes back to Erich Kahler's analysis of the English 18th century novel. See E. Kahler, "Die Verinnerung des Erzählens", *Die Neue Rundschau*, I:4 (1957), 501–546; II:1 (1959), 1–54; III:2 (1959), 177–220; English Translation: E. Kahler, *The Inward Turn of Narrative*, translated from the German by R. and C. Winston (Princeton, 1973).

The comic effect which results from the conflict between a prescribed religious way of life and a very wordly vitality is enhanced by the narrator's comment which approves of the Monk's mentality:

> And I seyde his opinion was good.
> What sholde he studie and make hymselven wood,
> Upon a book in cloystre alwey to poure,
> Or swynken with his handes, and laboure,
> As Austyn bit? How shal the world be served?
> Lat Austyn have his swynk to hym reserved!
>
> (I (A) 183–188)

How much authorial irony is hidden in these words must remain open to conjecture, i.e. we must ask ourselves if the author makes his narrator feign approval in order to criticize all the more satirically the secularization of the monks. It is possible, however, that Chaucer indeed agreed with his narrator and joined in his criticism of all the constraints which came with a spiritual culture, speaking as the advocate of 'natura' through his comedy. Whatever decision one makes in the interpretation of the lines quoted above, it is obvious that Chaucer refers to a historical change when he portrays tensions which produce comedy:

> This ilke Monk leet olde thynges pace,
> And heeld after the newe world the space.
>
> (I (A) 175–176)

When we said at the beginning of this analysis, in accordance with Stierle, that the object of comicality is that which threatens (or questions) a culture as a system, then this threat or questioning must be placed in a historical context. In the tensions between chivalry and bourgeoisie, between a world-denying and a wordly attitude, one becomes aware of an extensive historical change. The medieval order of life, in its secular, aristocratic and spiritual aspects, is replaced by a new concept of the world and of life which is decidedly orientated towards the here and now and which is governed by the bourgeoisie and its pragmatic attitude. At the waning of the Middle Ages, "when 'olde thynges pace'", there were various overlappings in the behaviour and the consciousness of the people, overlappings which showed at once the limitations of the old norms and the value of the new ones, but also the limitations of the new phenomena which were as yet not fully developed, and the subtle perfection and refined intellectuality of the old systems. Chaucer reacted to this interplay of cultural values and systems with his artistic instrument of narrative comedy. From humorous and sympathetic asides to direct satirical attacks, he used all the narrative devices he could summon in order to enable his audience to gain insight into the complexity of their own age, their consciousness and their nature. Thus, he met his own demand which he placed, as it were programmatically, at the end of the prologue to the *Canterbury Tales*: he presented "Tales of best sentence and moost solaas" (I (A) 798) for the enjoyment of his contemporaries as well as of a modern audience.

Versions of Comedy in Chaucer's *Canterbury Tales*

Derek Pearsall

Anyone who offers to speak on 'comedy' in the comic masterpiece of our greatest English comic poet would be well advised to be wary, and perhaps better advised to speak on something else, since there is inevitably the uneasy feeling that to speak of Chaucer on comedy is somehow to be implicated in it. Furthermore, comedy, although it is not to be identified with laughter, is certainly associated with it, and explaining what makes us laugh is a dogged kind of activity, it might appear, and no fun. As Chesterton says, "while the poet is always large and humorous, the critics are often small and serious",[1] and, though to be large and serious might not be too bad, nor even to be small and humorous, no-one wants to appear small and serious. There are other reasons too for being cautious in approaching such a subject as Chaucerian comedy, especially in association with laughter and humour, and, indeed, the warning given by the nineteenth-century French historian, Louis Cazamian, might seem to prohibit one from talking about the subject at all:

> Modern humour hardly came into its
> own till the Renascence; prior to that
> time, the mental complexity which it
> requires was not very widely diffused.[2]

However, we shall have to consider this remark, even coming from a Frenchman, as an impertinence.

At this point, it might be sensible to attempt some examination of the assumptions we make in thinking about comedy, and about humour, and the influence they are likely to have in our response to Chaucer. On the one hand, there is a general impression that the Middle Ages disapproved of comedy, at least of the kind that provokes laughter. "Christ is crucified – and dost thou laugh?" asked St. John Chrysostom[3], not anticipating much debate on the

---

1. G.K. Chesterton, *Chaucer* (London 1932), p. 20.
2. L. Cazamian, *The Development of English Humor* (New York 1930), p. 2, quoted by J.S.P. Tatlock,"Mediaeval Laughter", *Speculum*, 21 (1946), 289–94 (p. 290).
3. St. John Chrysostom, quoted by B. White,"Medieval Mirth", *Anglia*, 78 (1960), 284–301 (p. 290).

matter, and the exegetes were accustomed to point out with some satisfaction that Christ, though he is represented in the gospels as weeping, never laughed. Luke 6:25 is glossed by Bede and others as a condemnation of laughing[4], and Langland's Holy Church speaks of *filius dei* as he

> That neuere lyede ne lauhede in al his lyf-tyme.[5]

Dante's title for his great Christian poem is a deliberate appropriation of the term 'comedy', with its implications of literary form and its potentiality for laughter, to the demonstration of a divine providence in which comedy and tragedy, laughter and weeping, are alike transcended. The impossibility of human comedy, of laughter, within Dante's poem is starkly evident: it has been eliminated.

Within this context, comedy, as a literary form, has a precarious existence. To be allowed at all, it must be didactic, and the Middle Ages, as far as the official sponsors of its culture went, was content to acquiesce in the classical definition of comedy as a socially and morally normative form, working through the ridicule of vice and folly to the correction of deviancy. Laughter is not the purpose of comedy: as Ben Jonson, equally the inheritor of the classical tradition, says, "The moving of laughter is not always the end of comedy".[6] Laughter is, however, a concomitant of comedy, and the means to a kind of catharsis: a small dose of laughter, conceived of as in itself a meaningless *rictus*, expels those unsocial tendencies of which excessive laughter may be the symptom. This homeopathic view of comedy is essentially that expressed also in the classic nineteenth-century theorising of Meredith and Bergson.[7] Both reiterate the idea that comic laughter is the means through which vice and folly are ridiculed, and ostracized from the body of society. "The use of comedy", says Meredith, "is in teaching the world to understand what ails it" (p.13), and its "natural prey" is folly (p.33). In a characteristi-

---

4. See Bede in J.P. Migne (ed.), *Patrologia Latina*, vol. 92, col. 404, and the *Glossa Ordinaria* in *Patrologia Latina*, vol. 114, col. 263.
5. *Piers Plowman, by William Langland: An Edition of the C-text*, ed. D. Pearsall, passus II, line 32. See further the note to this line in that edition, p. 56.
6. "Nor, is the moving of laughter alwaies the end of *Comedy*, that is rather a fowling for the peoples delight, or their fooling. For, as *Aristotle* saies rightly, the moving of laughter, is a fault in Comedie, a kind of turpitude..." From *Timber, or Discoveries*, in the edition of Ben Jonson by C.H. Herford and P. and E. Simpson, Vol. VIII (Oxford, 1947), p. 643.
7. G. Meredith, "An Essay on Comedy" (first published 1877) and H. Bergson, "Laughter" (first published in French in 1900) are cited below from the convenient collection, *Comedy*, ed. W. Sypher (Garden City, N.J., 1956).

cally fastidious way, Meredith distinguishes the kind of laughter evoked by 'true comedy': "The test of true comedy is that it shall awaken thoughtful laughter" (p. 47). The 'belly-laugh', clearly, has no place in this polite world of comedy. Comedy, in fact, is a form of satire, milder and more devious, but still essentially moral in function, and thereby distinguished from 'humour':

> The comic differs from satire in not
> sharply driving into the quivering sensibilities,
> and from humour in not comforting them and
> tucking them up. (p. 43)

Bergson also speaks of a socio-medical function for comedy, isolating vanity as the principal ailment to which it is directed: "The specific remedy for vanity is laughter, and the one failing that is essentially laughable is vanity" (p. 173). Bergson has a keen perception of one of the important motor agents in laughter:

> We laugh every time a person gives us
> the impression of being a thing (p. 97)
> Any arrangement of acts and events is comic
> which gives us, in a single combination, the
> illusion of life and the distinct impression
> of a mechanical arrangement. (p. 105)

However, this physiological response is interpreted essentially as the means to the correction of antisocial behaviour:

> There is a certain rigidity of body,
> mind and character that society would
> like to get rid of in order to obtain
> from its members the greatest possible
> degree of elasticity and sociability.
> This rigidity is the comic, and laughter
> is its corrective. (pp. 73–4)

By these means, then, laughter is deodorised and made a source of moral uplift.

At the opposite extreme, and present in some form at any rate to the Middle Ages, there is the recognition that laughter is the essentially human and humanising act, the act through which humans assert their humanity. "Of all living creatures only man is endowed with laughter",[8] said Aristotle (not, apparently, having heard the Texan grackle), and the Middle Ages inherited

---

8. Aristotle, *On the Parts of Animals*, Book III, chapter 10.

this piece of wisdom as more or less self-evident. The definition of the nature of man commonly included a reference to the capacity for laughter:

Homo est animal rationale, mortale, risus capax.[9]

However, the larger implications of this unique capacity are commonly left unexamined and rarely emerge in literary or intellectual accounts of the function of laughter. The nearest approach is in clinical assessments of the therapeutic or recreational function of laughter, of which Olson has written so well in his recent book on the subject,[10] and of which the following might be taken as a representative, if itself rather bizarre example:

It is helpful for a leech
to have a stock of good tales and
honest that may make the patients
laugh, as well from the Bible as
from other tragedies ...[11]

However, the absence of explicit recognition of any more important function for laughter does not, of course, mean that it did not perform that function, and the book by Mikhail Bakhtin, *Rabelais and his World*,[12] vividly recreates a medieval world in which unofficial laughter constantly subverted official orthodoxies:

Laughter, which had been eliminated
in the Middle Ages from official cult and
ideology, made its unofficial but almost
legal nest under the shelter of almost
every feast. (p. 82)

Bakhtin goes on to describe the anti-authoritarian nature of such laughter:

The serious aspects of class culture
are official and authoritarian; they are
combined with violence, prohibitions,
limitations and always contain an element

9. Notker III (Labeo), *De Definitione*, quoted by H. Adolf, "On Mediaeval Laughter", *Speculum*, 22 (1947), 251–3 (p. 251). One might add a perhaps 'unmedieval' gloss: "and necessarily *risus capax* since both *rationale* and *mortale*". Laughter, as Kierkegaard says, (quoted in Sypher, *op. cit.*, p. 196), is the perception of contradiction.
10. G. Olson, *Literature as Recreation in the Later Middle Ages* (Ithaca and London, 1982).
11. J. Arderne, *Treatises of Fistula in Ano*, ed. D'Arcy Power, E. E. T. S., O.S. 139 (1910), p. 8, quoted in the translation provided by B. White, "Medieval Mirth", *Anglia*, 78 (1960), 284–301 (p. 285).
12. M. Bakhtin, *Rabelais and his World*, trans. (from the original Russian) by H. Iswolsky (Cambridge, Mass., 1965).

> of fear and intimidation ...
> Laughter, on the contrary, overcomes fear
> for it knows no inhibitions, no limitations.
> Its idiom is never used by violence and
> authority. (p. 122)

He associates it further with the regenerative power of what he was later to call the 'dialogic' imagination:

> True ambivalent and universal laughter
> does not deny seriousness but purifies and
> completes it. Laughter purifies from
> dogmatism, from the intolerant and the pet-
> rified; it liberates from fanaticism and
> pedantry, from fear and intimidation, from
> didacticism, naïveté and illusion, from the
> single meaning, the single level, from
> sentimentality. (pp. 122–3)

It is not difficult, incidentally, to recognise here the source of Umberto Eco's cunning murder-plot in *The Name of the Rose*, which focuses on the orthodox church's fanatical desire to keep secret the fact that Aristotle's lost discourse on Comedy in the *Poetics* had actually survived.

Such then are the assumptions which act as the poles between which speculation and analysis will flow. They will provide a context now for a more detailed consideration of Chaucerian comedy based on specific analysis of the structure and expectations of the six tales (or six-and-a-bit, if one includes the unfinished *Cook's Tale*) which are commonly classified as fabliaux – though it will emerge that there are qualifications to be made of this classification in respect of two of the six, the *Friar's* and *Summoner's Tales* (the others being the *Miller's, Reeve's, Merchant's* and *Shipman's Tales*). Comedy, of course, is present in a number of other tales, and pervasive in the links between them, those great masterpieces of comic dramatic writing, but the purpose here is to concentrate on the comic tale or fabliau as a specifically definable genre. It is accepted here that Jauss is right, in his "Theory of Genres", in asserting that consciousness of genre is fundamental to the successful reading experience:

> It is unimaginable that a literary
> work set itself into an informational
> vacuum, without indicating a specific
> situation of understanding. To this
> extent, every work belongs to a genre –
> whereby I mean neither more nor less than
> that for each work a preconstituted horizon

> of expectations must be ready at hand (this
> can also be understood as a relationship of
> 'rules of the game' ...).[13]

Recognition of genre is necessary if we are to steer a successful path between what Jauss calls "the Scylla of nominalist skepticism that allows only for a posteriori classifications and the Charybdis of regression into timeless typologies" (p. 78). More simply, as Burrow has pointed out, we have no notion of what a poem is for or about if we have no 'horizon of expectation' or sense of genre.[14] What, then, are the rules of the narrative game we are being invited to play in the Chaucerian fabliaux?

The rules of time and place are obvious. The time is the present, and the tale is offered as a report on contemporary life. It may begin with "Whilom", but there is no mention of "th'olde dayes" (as in the *Wife of Bath's Tale*, III, 857),[15] nor of what "olde stories tellen us" (*Knight's Tale*, I, 859). The place is likewise the familiar homely environment of town or village, with a special insistence by Chaucer on the English settings of the *Miller's*, *Reeve's* and *Cook's Tales* in Oxford, Cambridge (Trumpington being "nat fer fro Cantebrigge", *Reeve's Tale*, I, 3921) and London ("oure citee", *Cook's Tale,* I, 4365). The *Friar's Tale* is set in "my contree" (III, 1301) and the *Summoner's Tale* in Holderness in Yorkshire (III, 1710). The location of the *Shipman's Tale* in "Seint-Denys" (VII, 1), with further action in Paris and Bruges, would be a good deal less than exotic for a fourteenth-century English audience (and quite different from the romantic setting, elsewhere in France, of the *Franklin's Tale*). The *Merchant's Tale*, in this as in many other respects, is exceptional, in being set in Pavia in Italy: it may be that this gave an appropriately false grandeur or perverted glamour to what followed, and it is possible that Pavia had some kind of contemporary reputation as a 'city of sin', a kind of medieval Hamburg.[16]

13. H.R. Jauss, "The Theory of Genres and Medieval Literature" in *Toward an Aesthetic of Reception*, trans. (from the original German) by T. Bahti (Minneapolis, 1982), p. 79.
14. J.A. Burrow, "Poems Without Contexts: The Rawlinson Lyrics", *Essays in Criticism*, 29 (1979), 6–32. Reprinted in the author's *Essays on Medieval Literature* (Oxford, 1984), pp. 1–26. See also the same author's *Medieval Writers and Their Work: Middle English Literature and its Background, 1100–1500* (Oxford, 1982), p. 85: "Recognition of genre is not merely an academic exercise: it is an indispensable condition of understanding."
15. Quotations from Chaucer are from *The Complete Works of Geoffrey Chaucer*, ed. F.N. Robinson, 2nd. edn. (Cambridge, Mass., 1957).
16. See P.A. Olson, "The Merchant's Lombard Knight", *TSLL*, 3 (1961), 259–63; E. Brown, "Why Was Januarie Born 'Of Pavye'?" *NM*, 71 (1970), 654–8.

The social setting of fabliau is likewise firmly fixed. It is the world of the petit-bourgeois that is described, or, if that term means little in relation to medieval social and economic life, the world of tradespeople, usually thriving and aspirant. The tone of voice adopted in the description of this world, when it is allowed to come through, is one of patrician condescension or contempt, appropriate to the analysis of the behaviour of the inhabitants of a zoo. It is not, be it noted, the poorest classes who constitute the subject matter of these tales (except for the brief appearance of the old widow of the *Friar's Tale*, III, 1573): a fabliau set in a hovel would lose much of its piquancy, and, of course, a fabliau set in an aristocratic court would be a failed romance. (The *Merchant's Tale*, where the central character is, exceptionally, a knight, is well on its way towards this more enigmatic genre). Aspiration after status and recognition is common amongst the bourgeoisie of the fabliaux, and there is no lack of money. Nevertheless, the husband of the *Miller's Tale*, though he is a "riche gnof" (I, 3188), is still a "gnof", and the possession of money, so far from being an indication of superiority, is commonly scorned. The tone is unmistakable in the opening account of the merchant in the *Shipman's Tale*,

> That riche was, for which men helde hym wys.
> (VII, 2)

More explicit still, and acutely revealing of the implied social attitudes of fabliau, is the remark at the end of the description of Alysoun in the *Miller's Tale*:

> She was a prymerole, a piggesnye,
> For any lord to leggen in his bedde,
> Or yet for any good yeman to wedde.
> (I, 3268—70)

Such a comment, with its almost perceptible curling of the upper lip, makes one recognise the validity of Nykrog's argument that fabliaux are basically an aristocratic taste.[17] Indeed, the systematic belittling of bourgeois ignorance and stupidity in the fabliaux makes it surprising that they were ever associated with the lower classes of society, except as a reflex of that comfortable opinion that low moral standards are to be associated with the lower classes. At the same time, one must accept the further qualification of Nykrog's view made by Muscatine:

17. P. Nykrog, *Les Fabliaux: Etude d'histoire littéraire et de stylistique médiévale* (Copenhagen, 1957). Nykrog revised the traditional view put forward by J. Bédier, *Les Fabliaux* (Paris, 1893), that they were essentially bourgeois in origin.

> We cannot speak of simple, homogeneous
> social classes, nor of simple social attitudes,
> in discussing fabliau origins or audiences.[18]

One would have to accept, too, that Chaucer has wonderfully complicated our response to his fabliaux by having them told, in the *Canterbury Tales*, not by aristocratic young men, as in the *Decameron*, but by the kind of people they are about. By this means, as Burrow says, "Chaucer blurs the distinction between the fiction of the pilgrimage and the fictions which it encloses", and creates of those "rich confusions" that he loved to exploit.[19]

There are other elements in the structure of the fabliaux that might be elicited as defining the expectations of the genre, but the most important, as yet unmentioned, is the nature of the ideological contract into which the audience of such tales is expected to enter with the author, the assumptions that we are asked to share. In romance, to take a contrasting type of tale, we are asked to share in the belief and accept for the purposes of the story that there are noble ideals of behaviour, fidelity to which is the means through which human existence is validated, through which life is shown to be meaningful. So Arviragus speaks of "trouthe" (*Franklin's Tale*, V, 1479), and Arcite, in dying, of "trouthe, honour, knyghthede" and the other values he has neglected in his living (*Knight's Tale*, I, 2789). In religious tales and saints' legends, an equally self-transcending system of values operates, in this case proving the significance of life through the demonstration of its ultimate insignificance in relation to life eternal. Chaucerian comedy sets all this aside, and asserts that there are no values, secular or religious, more important than survival and the satisfaction of appetite. Characters who may be temporarily under the illusion that things are otherwise, such as Absolon or January, are given short shrift. The injunction is not 'Be noble', or 'be good', but 'be smart'. Our extreme satisfaction in seeing Nicholas, in the *Miller's Tale*, receive his 'come-uppance' is not based on a perception of moral justice being done — the idea that he is "scalded in the towte" (I, 3853) because he has committed adultery is too trite for words — but on the comic 'justice' of 'the biter bit'. Nicholas makes himself vulnerable because he ceases to be smart, and tries to play the same trick on Absolon that Alysoun has already played: this is not the behaviour of a cunning animal, which is what the comic hero is expected to be.

18. C. Muscatine, "The Social Background of the Old French Fabliaux", *Genre*, 9 (1976), 1–19 (p. 18).
19. J.A. Burrow, *Medieval Writers and Their Work: Middle English Literature and its Background 1100–1500* (Oxford, 1982), p. 80.

It will be seen that Chaucerian comedy, on this definition of it, differs markedly from comedy as classically defined, that is, as a socially and morally
normative literary form, working to correct our behaviour through making us
laugh at the ridiculousness of vice and folly. If one asked what were the social
and moral norms towards which Chaucerian comedy worked, it would be
difficult to return any simple answer, or any complicated one for that matter.
So far from being clearly displayed, the social and moral norms are often
openly subverted. For the critics to reassert their centrality by attributing the
neglect or subversion of moral value to the inadequacy of the pilgrim-narrator
is a well established modern ploy,[20] but it is based on a misunderstanding of
the rules of this particular game. This is not to say, of course, that satire, done
from well-recognised normative positions, is not present in these comic tales:
the complacency and gullibility of John the Carpenter, the inane vanity and
self-regard of Absolon, are classics of satirical comedy. They are, as Meredith
would say, "the natural prey of the Comic".[21] But the tales as a whole are not
satirical comedies: their reference beyond themselves is by virtue of the genre
to which they belong, and not through their own literal content. The *Friar's*
and *Summoner's Tales* might seem to constitute an exception here, since they
are certainly satirical anecdotes, and there is no doubt that we are to regard
the behaviour of the summoner of the *Friar's Tale* and the friar of the *Summoner's Tale* as wicked. Yet even here the satire is made part of a mutual exchange of abuse and thereby pushed away from any authoritative moral
centre. The wickedness of summoners and friars remains the theme of the
two tales, respectively, but not their *point*.

At the same time that one rejects moralistic interpretations of Chaucerian
comedy, it would be a misreading of Bakhtin to claim for the tales an alternative kind of assertiveness as a 'celebration of life', a universal subversion of
established values. In a certain basic way, of course, laughter does offer a kind
of psychic release, especially when we laugh at the blaspheming of what is re-
vered, the open practice of verbal obscenity, the explicit depiction of excre-
tory and sexual functions, and this is well recognised in modern accounts of
the function of comedy:

> Comedy is a momentary and publicly
> useful resistance to authority and an

20. There are good examples in P.A. Olson, "*The Reeve's Tale:* Chaucer's *Measure for
Measure*", *SP*, 59 (1962), 1–17; and *ibid*., "Chaucer's Merchant and January's
' Hevene in erthe heere' ", *ELH*, 28 (1961), 203–213.
21. Meredith, "An Essay on Comedy", in Sypher, *Comedy* (see note 7 above), p. 33.

> escape from its pressures; and its mechanism
> is a free discharge of repressed psychic
> energy or resentment through laughter.[22]

This assertion of vitality, however, has no 'meaning' beyond itself, nor does the emphasis on physicality make comedy more significant, for it would be crass to be tempted into believing that physical functions are more 'real' than intellectual, emotional, or spiritual functions. Chaucer's comic tales exist no more to celebrate life than to criticise immorality: the narrative assumptions we are asked to make are no more realistic, have no more relation to the real world, than those of romance.

At this point, it is appropriate to allow the *Friar's* and *Summoner's Tales* to detach themselves from the main group, as they have often threatened to do in the preceding paragraphs, and to appropriate the term *fabliau* more strictly to the four remaining tales. It will be seen that these four have a very close generic identity, being not only comic tales of low life involving trickery (the broad definition of fabliau), but all of them having to do with marital and sexual relations. In fact, all of them are tales in which a bourgeois husband is duped or tricked into conniving at the free award of his wife's sexual favours to a clever young man. This structure may seem well enough defined, but the model can be refined even further.

The persons required are three, a husband, a wife, and an 'intruder', though the functions of the last two may be duplicated in the more complex plots. The 'intruder' is always a man: a modern fabliau might have a woman, but not a medieval one. The husband belongs to the world of trade, except in the *Merchant's Tale*, where he is a knight. The wife is younger than her husband, or, if not younger, still with some unsatisfied sexual potential. This is briefly and devastatingly indicated, for instance, in an aside in the *Reeve's Tale*, when John leaps on the good wife:

> So myrie a fit ne hadde she nat ful yoore;
> (I, 4230)

The wife of the *fabliaux* is not, it must be stressed, promiscuous, and there is no suggestion that the affair in which she is at present engaged is a matter of regular occupation. This is not because Chaucer is mealy-mouthed where Boccaccio is (quite often) frank, but because he can thereby increase the amount and quality of the intrigue. The 'intruder' is usually younger than the hus-

22. W. Sypher, "The Social Meanings of Comedy", in Sypher, *Comedy*, p. 243.

band, or at least, as in the *Shipman's Tale*, explicitly more sexually active. More importantly, he belongs to a different class, being usually a student or other kind of cleric or religious, and, therefore, more clever, flexible and mobile than those with whom he is temporarily (as lodger or guest) accommodated. He is a member of a classless intellectual elite who, in being shown as a predator upon the conventional marital and materialistic values of the bourgeois, can be brought into an implicit alliance with the aristocracy. The *Merchant's Tale* is once more the exception, and there is no doubt that the nastiness of the tale is much increased by the fact that the intruder is a squire of January's own household, and furthermore one who plays a subordinate part in the intrigue to the wife.

It is not difficult to speak of Chaucer's fabliaux in this way, with the plot-elements and characters abstracted as functions, and it is not a distortion of the nature of the fabliaux to draw attention to the narrative rules upon which they operate. But the success of Chaucer's poetry is in the manner in which he works variations on these set patterns, defies expectation, tests the tolerance of the form and the habitual perceptions of the reader, and creates four poems which are as enjoyable for the ways in which each is unique as for the ways in which they fit a pattern.

The *Miller's Tale*, for instance, is distinctive for the genial gusto with which it is told. The events are as nasty and painful as they usually are in a fabliau, but there is about the whole tale an unparalleled *joie de vivre*. It is characteristic of the tale that the love-making of Nicholas and Alysoun, when they come tripping down the step-ladders from the wooden tubs that Alysoun's husband has so carpenter-like prepared, is not described, only alluded to, and in these terms:

> Ther was the revel and the melodye;
> (I, 3652)

It is one of many allusions to music in the tale, and, combined with the hilarious travesty of courtly idealism in Absolon's ludicrous philandering, contributes to its lyrical, almost Illyrian quality. The tale is also, by contrast, a *tour de force* of circumstantiality. Every detail is vividly realised — the hole in the door of Nicholas's room for the cat to come in and out of and for the servant, Robyn, to peer in at, the church windows carved in the buckles of Absolon's shoes, the window in the attic gable out of which the tubs will float when the flood rises — and the background of the narrative is likewise drawn in with graphic strokes — Gervase the blacksmith at work in his forge at night, the carpenter's commissions for the local abbey at Oseney, the frequent references to urban performance of the local mystery plays — so that we have a sense of life going on continuously behind the story. The characters are done with extraordinary fullness and richness, and with an unexpected generosity: John's concern for his lodger and his wife is as genuinely part of his old fool's nature as his ignorance and complacency, while Nicholas, endearingly, seems to get as excited about imagining the working-out of his fantastically complex plot as he does about Alysoun. The ending is sublime: there are few moments in narrative so perfect as our sudden realisation that Nicholas's cry for water (I, 3815) will make the carpenter, long-forgotten in his tub, think that the flood has come and cut the rope and come crashing down.

The *Reeve's Tale*, by contrast, has a sour taste. The setting is similarly substantial, but the elements of lyricism have gone, and the whole tale has the air of being calculated and engineered to humiliate the Miller. The portrait of the miller at the beginning sets him up deliberately as a target to be shot at; his wife and daughter are scornfully and diminishingly described; and the two students are oafish simpletons whose crudity throws into even sharper relief the miller's stupidity in allowing himself to be outwitted by them. The couplings in the night are acts of vindictiveness rather than desire, and are described in language that gives no access to pleasure or feeling of any kind. Much of the bitterness is dissipated in the farcical *allegro con brio* of the final bedroom scene,[23] but there remains an undertone of distastefulness. It is partly that our laughter is given an edge of uneasiness by the fact that we have to share it with the malicious Reeve, and Chaucer can be seen here giving added indirection and complexity to the fabliau form, incorporating traditional satirical elements and yet, in showing them to be the product of an alienated intelligence, not allowing us any comfortable moral judgements. But the *Reeve's Tale* has, above all, to be read with the *Miller's Tale*. They are inseparable, the Jekyll and Hyde of fabliau.

The *Shipman's Tale* is the quietest of the fabliaux. There is no violence, no lyrical fantasies or courtly extravagance, and no-one is much put out by what happens. The scene between the wife and the monk in the garden is an almost completely decorous comedy of manners, and the conversations between the monk and the husband are masterpieces of bonhomie. No criticism is offered of a world in which sex and money can be so conveniently exchanged, except

---

23. Farce, it has been well observed, is "comedy with the meaning left out". See L.J. Potts, *Comedy* (London, 1948), p. 152, quoted by A. Rodway, *English Comedy: Its Role and Nature from Chaucer to the Present Day* (London, 1975), p. 31.

such as is present in reporting such a world without comment, and the characters are portrayed with a deceptive blandness. Hardly a ripple disturbs the surface, but there is considerable depth of insight in the tale into the motives of those who are avaricious less of gain than of the reputation of not being avaricious, and less of success than of the reputation of being successful. The tale is exhilarating in its challenge to the familiar decencies of social intercourse.

Of the *Merchant's Tale*, it is impossible to speak at once briefly and adequately. It is the tale in which Chaucer threatens to explode fabliau into a new dimension of 'black comedy'. Every line drips with contempt and sneering malevolence, and January is a disgusting portrait of senile lust in which Chaucer, by some exercise of the Thersitean imagination, endows the usual innuendoes of fabliau with a repulsive physical actuality. He does more: he grants to January a kind of deformed moral consciousness which stimulates in him and in us impulses towards feeling and moral reflection quite alien to the genre of fabliau. Even the young lovers (the phrase is sick, in the context) are reptilian in the calculating coldness of their sexuality, and the images that stick in one's mind — the love-letter in the privy, Damian fawning upon January, crouching beneath a bush in the garden — are those of a diseased imagination. The ending, with the ridiculous coupling in the pear-tree, restores some of the briskness and spiritedness of fabliau, but a sense of trespass in the tale as a whole remains. Chaucer, in suggesting to us all sorts of themes of moral and emotional significance, violates the expectations of the genre without creating any alternative order for the understanding of the tale. A character called Justinus appears, and might be expected, from his name, to hold the key, but his wisdom is only that of embittered cynicism, and he emerges as a part of the disorder of the tale, not a corrective to it.

The *Friar's* and *Summoner's Tales* have already been distinguished as to content from the four tales of sexual intrigue, but, though they are not strictly speaking fabliaux, they operate according to the same basic comic rules. Here, as there, the criterion by which human beings are to be judged is the extent to which they find means fully to satisfy the appetites of their nature, and to bend the world by clever manipulation to the rapaciousness of their will. Chaucer absorbs traditional satire of the professional activities of summoners and friars into the dramatic comedy of the exchange of abuse between the Friar and the Summoner, so that, while moral outrage on our part at what they describe each other as doing is a necessary preliminary response, it is eventually swallowed up in laughter, since what the narrators do is to prove not that their victims are knaves, but that they are fools. To be portrayed as successfully wicked is something of a compliment, in this world of values; contempt and ridicule are far more painful than moral condemnation. The victims of both tales are portrayed, therefore, as pathetically gullible. They misunderstand things that would be obvious to the meanest intelligence, mistake the surface for the reality, the letter for the spirit, and end up in defeat because of their own stupidity.

Nothing could be more ridiculous than the summoner's failure to understand the true nature of the yeoman he meets, or to respond to the many heavy hints he gets, or to appreciate the full significance of the situation in which he finds himself. Our sympathy goes out to the yeoman-devil, who begins to evince a certain understandable exasperation at having been sent out on a special mission to capture a soul of such banality. Through all the conversation with the yeoman-devil, and the subsequent incidents with the carter and the old widow, the summoner remains impervious to any perception but that of the grossly literal. Twice invited to think again or to repent (III, 1521, 1629), he seems not even to understand what he stands to lose. The joke against him is not that he is snatched off to hell, but that he probably will not even realise where he is when he gets there. So too with the friar in the *Summoner's Tale*: he has shown himself an accomplished master of hypocrisy in the course of the tale, with an almost Falstaffian skill in getting out of tricky situations, but when he falls over-eagerly into Thomas's trap he seems, ridiculously, more put out by the absurdly impossible problem in *ars-metrike* he has been set than by the grossness of his humiliation. All our memory of the quarrel between the Friar and the Summoner, all possibility of morally based satire on the friar, seems swallowed up in the posing of this puzzle of the divided fart and its ingeniously fantastic solution.

It would be possible to argue that the representation of the victims as stupid makes these two tales successful as satires, but the displacement of satire from its moral centre, and the involvement of the two narrators in the acts of judgement that are being made, makes this position untenable. Who would want to share a platform with the Friar or the Summoner? Certainly, the turning of the villain into a buffoon has a potential moral implication, if only, as Nabokov says, because "crime is a sorry farce whether the stressing of this may help the community or not". He goes on:

> The twinkle in the author's eye as he
> notes the imbecile drooping of a murderer's
> underlip, or watches the stumpy forefinger
> of a professional tyrant exploring a profit-
> able nostril in the solitude of his sumptuous

> bedroom, this twinkle is what punishes your
> man more surely than the pistol of a tip-
> toeing conspirator.[24]

Chaucer seems to be beyond this, even to a kind of complicity with the creatures of his comedy that declares them almost immune from orthodox moral criticism. The world he enables us to perceive is not a world in which we are allowed to patronise lesser beings, but one in which we are implicated and to which, with part of ourselves, we belong.

The Chaucerian comic tale, or fabliau in the broader sense, is obviously a partisan form, a kind of guerrilla warfare on established values. Its larger function can perhaps be best illustrated by further comparison with romance, since the two literary forms seem to exist in a complementary relationship. Romance asserts the possibility that men may behave in a noble and self-transcending manner; fabliau declares the certainty that they will always behave like animals. The one portrays men as superhuman, the other portrays them as subhuman. Neither is 'true' nor realistic, though we might say that our understanding of what *is* true gains depth from having different slanting lights thrown upon reality, so that beneficial shock, enrichment, invigoration is given to our perception of the world. Romance and fabliau complement one another, and Chaucer encourages us to look at them thus by setting the *Knight's Tale* and the *Miller's Tale* side by side. Each type of story makes a selection of human experience in accord with its own narrative conventions or rules. Out of the interlocking of these and other different types of story, in the general medieval hierarchy of genres, or in the *Canterbury Tales* as a whole, grows the social relevance of literary forms, the fabliau amongst them.

---

24. "The Art of Literature and Commonsense", in Vladimir Nabokov, *Lectures on Literature*, ed. F. Bowers (Weidenfeld and Nicolson, 1980; Picador, 1983), p. 376.

Chaucer's *Shipman's Tale* Within the Context of the French Fabliaux Tradition

Joerg O. Fichte

In contrast to the often divergent approaches taken to some of the *Canterbury Tales*, the criticism of the *Shipman's Tale* appears to be fairly homogeneous. The narrative belongs to the group of Chaucer's fabliaux; many critics believe it to be the most typical Chaucerian representation of this literary genre.[1] Following the leads provided by John W. Spargo, it is generally assumed that Chaucer drew from and reworked a French tale now lost.[2] This assumption is based primarily on the fact that of all Chaucer's fabliaux only the *Shipman's Tale* features a French setting. The action takes place in St. Denis in the vicinity of Paris.

Against the assignment of the *Shipman's Tale* to the corpus of Chaucer's fabliaux surely no objections can be raised; however, the assertion that it is Chaucer's most typical representative of the fabliaux genre has still to be tested. As is to be expected, some more recent Chaucerians have dedicated studies to a closer analysis of the *Shipman's Tale* within the context of the French fabliau tradition. Thus, Michael McClintock maintains: "Chaucer is indubitably working with an established genre, but he is not working within this genre."[3] And Peter Nicholson makes the juxtaposition of "two contrasting worlds of experience, one drawn from the fabliaux and one typically bourgeois" responsible for the poem's form.[4] Both critics base their estimates of the

1. J.A. Burrow, *A Reading of Sir Gawain and the Green Knight* (London, 1965), p. 74; C. Muscatine, "*The Canterbury Tales*: Style of the Man and Style of the Work", in D.S. Brewer (ed.), *Chaucer and Chaucerians* (Alabama, 1966), p. 105; D.A. Pearsall, "The Canterbury Tales", in W.F. Bolton (ed.), *The History of Literature in the English Language* (London, 1970), I, p. 187; T.D. Cooke, *The Old French and Chaucerian Fabliaux. A Study of Their Comic Climax* (Columbia & London, 1978), p. 172; D.S. Brewer, "The Fabliaux", in Beryl Rowland (ed.), *Companion to Chaucer Studies*, 2nd rev. ed. (New York & Oxford, 1979), p. 309.
2. J.W. Spargo, *Chaucer's Shipman's Tale: The Lover's Gift Regained* [Folklore Fellows Communications] No. 51 (Helsinki, 1930), p. 56.
3. M.W. McClintock, "Games and the Players of Games: Old French Fabliaux and the *Shipman's Tale*", *ChauR*, 5 (1970/71), 112.
4. P. Nicholson, "The 'Shipman's Tale' and the Fabliaux," *ELH*, 45 (1978), 586.

relationship of Chaucer's *Shipman's Tale* to the genre of the French fabliau on a set of criteria which they regard as characteristic of this literary form. Nicholson's approach is inductive, that is, he starts his analysis with the *Shipman's Tale* itself, enumerating all of those points which, in his opinion, deviate from the norms of the fabliau. Chaucer's tale, for instance, lacks "the accustomed bawdiness of the other fabliaux".[5] Instead "its most striking qualities are a pervasive verbal humor of a sort that does not occur in the French fabliaux".[6] Moreover, the development of the plot runs contrary to the audience's expectations. The encounter between the monk and the wife does not lead to an "assignation, but to the wife's request for a loan".[7] Unlike the conventional fabliau wife, the merchant's spouse in the *Shipman's Tale* must hide her debt, not her lovemaking.[8] And the adultery leads not to a conflict or disruption, but to a happy conclusion of the tale.[9] Finally, the narrator, who in Chaucer's other fabliaux immerses himself fully in the victimization of the characters, takes no explicit position at the expense of any of the literary personages in the *Shipman's Tale*.[10]

In contrast to Nicholson's inductive approach, McClintock takes a deductive one. First, he provides a definition of the fabliau, and then he investigates the deviations in the *Shipman's Tale* from the genre which he defines as follows: "The narrative values of the fabliaux are brevity and clarity ... Directed toward the generation of a particular and limited audience response – laughter – the fabliaux simply have not got the scope for the digressions that establish a 'round' character or for the complex, often ambiguous actions through which such characters are probed. The fabliaux are populated by types ... played off against each other in various cliché situations. A fabliau is specifically a kind of situation comedy."[11] Instead of dealing with all of these points in reference to the *Shipman's Tale*, though, McClintock concentrates his investigation on the playful element of the fabliau, that is, his analysis centers on the gaming or playing of games in Chaucer's tale.

Both investigations do not endeavor to cover the whole scope of the text, but are limited to the analysis of certain salient points within it. Thus, a detailled study of the *Shipman's Tale* within the context of the French fabliau tradi-

5. Ibid., p. 583.
6. Ibid., p. 583.
7. Ibid., p. 589.
8. Ibid., p. 589.
9. Ibid., p. 591.
10. Ibid., p. 594.
11. M.W. McClintock, p. 113.

tion has still to be undertaken. Such is the object of this paper, which also tries to bring to bear upon the study of Chaucer's handling of the traditional genre the findings made by a generation of scholars after Nykrog.[12] Their research enables us to present a much fuller and more accurate description of the fabliau genre by including such features as communicative situation, province of meaning, authorial intent and audience reception. It is now possible to establish a catalogue of characteristic features of the genre and to compare Chaucer's treatment of the fabliau in the *Shipman's Tale* with the hypothetical model which they describe.[13] Step one, therefore, must be the establishment of a register of genre markers and their meaningful arrangement within a system designed for the description and interpretation of poetic texts. The model to be devised must feature categories, moreover, which enable us both to analyse all texts and to distribute them to their respective literary genre, for the goal of the process is the establishment of a corpus of similar texts and the determination of the properties they have in common. In order to achieve this, I shall adopt the following hermeneutic procedure for the constitution of a corpus of fabliaux: after a survey of the mass of single works, I shall set up a class characterized by a certain group of invariant elements and I shall then trace the historical development of the resulting text corpus. In this way, the conditions will be met which are necessary for the analysis of single works in their relationship to the total corpus as well as for the transformational

12. J. Rychner, *Contribution a l'étude des fabliaux*, 2 vols. (Genève 1968); J. Beyer, *Schwank und Moral. Untersuchungen zum altfranzösischen Fabliau und verwandten Formen. Studia Romanica*, 16 (Heidelberg, 1969); P. Dronke, "The Rise of the Medieval Fabliau: Latin and Vernacular Evidence", *RE*, 85 (1973), 275–95; M.J. Schenck, "Functions and Roles in the Fabliau", *CL*, 30 (1975), 22–34 and "The Morphology of the Fabliau", *Fabula*, 17 (1976), 26–39; R.J. Pearcey, "Investigations into the Principles of Fabliau Structure", *Genre*, 9 (1976), 345–78; R. Kiesow, *Die Fabliaux. Zur Genese und Typologie einer Gattung der altfranzösischen Kurzerzählung* (Berlin, 1976); W. Noomen, "Structures narratives et force comique: Les Fabliaux", *Neophil*, 62 (1978), 361–73; T.D. Cooke, *The Old French and Chaucerian Fabliaux. A Study of Their Comic Climax*; P. Ménard, *Les Fabliaux. Contes à rire du Moyen Age* (Paris, 1983); and R.H. Bloch, *The Scandal of the Fabliaux* (Chicago & London, 1986).
13. Such a genre is to be distinguished from the *Schwank*, as understood by Jürgen Beyer, who regards the *Schwank* as the result of a reductive process, as a specific activity of the spirit that precedes the formation of any genre and that is not necessarily confined to the limitations of a certain genre. The fabliau in its various forms would then become the vessel that could receive and collect the multifarious expressions of the vernacular comic story (J. Beyer, pp. 10–12). As examples of *Schwank* literature the *comoedia elegiaca*, the nine *Schwank* fables of Marie de France, the eight examples of *Schwank* material in the *Disciplina clericalis*, and finally the *ridicula* or Latin *Schulschwänke* are discussed by Beyer in the subsequent chapters, pp. 18–93. For a similar approach see also P. Dronke, p. 291, who speaks

ability of the genre in regard to the specific forms of the single works. Such a dialectic procedure will facilitate modifications of the previously established model. Beyond this, authorial intent, if stated explicitly, and the conditions of reception, if ascertainable, will also have to be taken into consideration, since a text may either be assigned to a certain genre by its author or be understood as such by its audience.

A glance at the foremost collection of medieval French fabliaux by Anatole de Montaiglon and Gaston Raynaud demonstrates that there exists a large corpus of works dating from around 1200 to the beginning of the 14th century which are called "fabliau" by their authors. These make up about half of the body of works which Bédier, Nykrog, and the editors of *Le Nouveau Recueil Complet des Fabliaux* would assign to the fabliau canon.[14] Although some of these will not fit the model to be devised — they belong to other literary genres such as the *dit*, the *debat* or the *fable* —[15], about three quarters of the remaining corpus can be called *fabliaux proprement dits*. In short, the view of Zumthor or Tiemann, that the fabliau has never really existed as an independent genre but should be seen only within the larger context of the major genres of Old French brief narratives, can no longer be upheld in this peremptory fashion.[16] Rather, there must have been some consensus among the producers of literature in the 13th and 14th centuries that a literary form by the name of fabliau obeying certain laws existed and that an audience

of a "fabliau feeling" crystallizing in various places, where fabliaux became a literary fashion of a specific kind: "in tenth and eleventh century Germany, in a learned and possibly aristocratic milieu — fabliaux in lyric form; in mid-twelfth century France, in a learned milieu, fabliaux in classicizing and dramatic forms; in thirteenth century France, in a vernacular milieu — fabliaux in octosyllabic couplets; in thirteenth century Italy, again in a vernacular milieu — fabliaux in short-story form."

14. The estimate of what should be included in the canon of genuine fabliaux differs. J. Bédier, *Les Fabliaux. Études de littérature populaires et d'histoire littéraire du Moyen Age*, 4th rev. ed. (Paris, 1924), pp. 436–40 lists 147 tales; P. Nykrog, *Les Fabliaux. Nouvelle édition* (Genève, 1973), pp. 311–24 lists 160; and N. van den Boogard, "Le Nouveau Recueil Complet des Fabliaux", *Neophil*, 61 (1977), 342–44 lists 127. The collection by A. de Montaiglon and G. Raynaud, *Recueil Général et Complet des Fabliaux des XIIIe et XIVe Siècles*, 6 vols. (Paris, 1872–90), hereafter cited as *MR*, contains 152 specimens.

15. As R. Kiesow, pp. 30–42, observes, the reason why these pieces are called fabliau is their inclusion in manuscripts containing predominantly fabliaux. Also, many fabliaux go by the names of other literary genres such as the *conte, dit, ditié, example, fable, lai, proverbe, risée, roman*, and *truffe*.

16. P. Zumthor, *Histoire littéraire de la France médiévale (VIe – XIVe siècles)* (Paris, 1954), p. 239; and H. Tiemann, "Bemerkungen zur Entstehungsgeschichte der Fabliaux", *RR*, 72 (1960), 411.

hearing the term used in the introduction to a tale would have definite expectations about the form and nature of the story they were about to hear.[17] If one, moreover, compares the corpus of texts labelled fabliau with other literary genres, differences in conception and execution become readily apparent. Based on the analysis of the text corpus called *fabliaux proprement dits*, comprising roughly sixty specimens, a narrative model can be derived consisting of the following four major categories: communicative situation; province of meaning, subdivided into the aspects of world picture, agents, plot, space, time, and point of view; authorial intent; and audience reception.

The communicative situation is comprised of a sender, a message and a receiver of this message. The sender, often anonymous, can be either the author or an adaptor or a performer of the tale presented in either written or oral form to an audience of either listeners or readers who are looking for entertainment.

The narrative itself progresses towards a comic peripety which constitutes the climax of the fabliau.[18] The action narrated takes place in a world which is disordered and obeys no superior moral law. It is characterized by the total absence of any ideals or values to which the characters could aspire or by which they are guided. Rather, the characters impose their own law upon it — a law of selfishness, hedonism and deceit. Thus, they create their own world to suit their selfish interests. Devoid of a metaphysical dimension, the world becomes a playground of lustful hedonists and tricksters persuing a life of physical gratification. This total suspension of moral laws reduces the world to a mere stage on which man enacts his life as a farce.

In such a world the figures can only be one-dimensional, unindividualized types because subtle characterization and heterogeneity would break the narrow frame of the fabliau. What has been said here about the typicality and one-dimensionality of the figures applies, of course, also to the characteriza-

---

17. Cf. the prologue to *Du Chevalier qui fist les cons parler*, *MR*, VI, p. 68, ll. 1–11:
   Flabel sont or mout entorsé;
   Maint denier en ont enborsé
   Cil qui les content et les portent,
   Quar grant confortement raportent
   As enovrez et as oiseus,
   Quant il n'i a genz trop noiseus,
   Et nès à ceus qui sont plain d'ire,
   Si lor fait il grant alegance
   Et oublier duel et pesance,
   Et mauvaitié et pensement.
18. Cf. also T.D. Cooke, pp. 107–36.

tion found in other literary genres, such as the exemplum or the saint's life. Yet, the reason for their use of types is entirely different. In the exemplum the figures are one-dimensional because they support the exemplary plot, they illustrate its action, that is, they have a demonstrative function. And in the saint's life they are one-dimensional because they exemplify the paradigmatic experience of election, crisis or conversion, temptation or passion, and triumph. In both genres, therefore, the figures are a direct consequence of the world picture which they reflect, while in the fabliau the figures determine the amoral world picture of the genre. They not only support the plot but carry it, since the fabliau action can only exist because of the cast of characters employed. As Nykrog has shown, the agents in the fabliau come from all ranks of society but they rarely mingle, that is, the characters prefer to move in their own class.[19] This holds especially true for the members of the nobility, though tales featuring members of the aristocracy are the exception rather than the rule. The bulk of the characters is made up of bourgeois, villains, priests and clerks and tends to typify the class or estate conception. Also, the plot structure of the fabliau revolving around deceit adds to the necessity of having one-dimensional characters. The duper must be intellectually more astute – he therefore often belongs to the clergy – than the dupe who is usually a villain, that is, a peasant, an artisan, or a tradesman. Thus, a combination of class or estate conception and function produces typicality. Since the object of the duper's intention is often a woman connected to the dupe by family bonds – either his wife or his daughter –, she has to be characterized in such a way as to be amenable to the duper's designs, which are mostly sexual. She has to be available, willing, and wily or at least available, gullible and naive. If the woman is the duper herself, she has to be shrewd or intellectually and/or socially superior to her husband. Thus, again we arrive at a typicality necessary for the implementation of the plot.

In the preceding discussion of the figures and their characterization in their relationship to the world picture, occasional references to the plot structure of the fabliau were unavoidable. Although plot structure is not necessarily a totally reliable indicator of literary genres, it often happens that a genre features recurrent structural elements. A chivalric romance, for instance, no matter how intricate or loose its plot structure may be, needs the constitutive parts of either *aventure* or quest or both. A saint's legend must have the elements of temptation (also in the form of affliction) and triumph after a successful struggle. Without such key actions the plot of these two genres is in-

19. P. Nykrog, pp. 118–19.

complete. The fabliau, as I have indicated, revolves around deception or trickery, which can even take the form of self-deception, as in the fabliaux *De la Damoisele qui ne pooit oïr parler de foutre, De la Pucele qui abevra le polain*, and *De l'Escuiruel.*[20] The deception, finally, does not even need to be consciously employed. It can be the result of a misunderstanding, as in the tale *De la Male Honte.*[21] This process of deception demands a structure in which at least one peripety, that is, a change in fortune, takes place. An anagnorisis is not needed, however. As a matter of fact, there exist quite a number of fabliaux belonging to the type of "the husband beaten and content" where a moment of recognition does not occur, as for instance *De la Borgoise d'Orliens, De la Dame qui fist batre son mari* and *Romanz de un Chivaler et de sa dame et de un clerk.*[22] In short, anagnorisis is not the necessary consequence of the peripety; rather, the resolution can follow immediately after the change in fortune has occured. The basic plot structure would thus contain the following four elements: exposition, development of deceptive strategies, climax and peripety, and resolution. This base structure can, of course, be supplemented and amplified. There can be the element of anagnorisis and there can also be subsequent peripeties, if the dupe turns duper and develops deceptive counterstrategies to take revenge. Or the deception leading to the peripety can occur in a number of successive stages, as for instance in *Du Bouchier d'Abevile* or *Du Prestre et du chevalier.*[23]

Plot structure and the characters of the fabliau are also partially responsible for the treatment of space and time in this literary genre. The setting for the action we encounter is an everyday environment with a multiplicity of ordinary human activities. The emphasis lies on the familiarity of the surroundings with which the audience is intimately acquainted. To evoke this impression of familiarity, fabliau authors utilize a few "stage props" which characterize the milieu. However, utensils, furniture, tools, and even pieces of clothing are not solely employed for the sake of authenticating realism; they are also used for functional purposes: they promote the plot.[24] Thus, the appearance of realis-

20. *MR*, III, pp. 81–85 and *MR*, V, pp. 24–31; *MR*, IV, pp. 199–207; *MR*, V, pp. 101–08.
21. *MR*, IV, pp. 4–46 and *MR*, V, pp. 95–100.
22. *MR*, I, pp. 117–25; *MR*, IV, pp. 133–43; *MR*, II, pp. 215–34.
23. *MR*, III, pp. 227–46; *MR*, II, pp. 46–91.
24. Cf. the tub in *Le Cuvier, MR*, I, pp. 126–31; the cradle in *De Gombert et des .II. clers, MS*, I, pp. 238–44 and *Le Meunier et les .II. clers, MR*, V, pp. 83–94; the tools in Connebert's forge in *De Connebert, MR*, V, pp. 160–70; the petticoat in *Le Dit dou pliçon, MR*, VI, pp. 260–63 and the breeches in *Des Braies le priestre, MR*, VI, pp. 257–60.

tic details in typical fabliaux occurs only sparingly because their authors are usually interested in strict economy.[25]

The same economy, incidentally, is also observable in the treatment of time. Since the fabliau action, compressed into an average of 250 lines, progresses swiftly towards its climax and peripety, the development appears rapid, often even precipitous. Narrative and narrated time are usually reduced to the absolute minimum. There are few or no digressions; rather, the interest of the narrator centers on the speedy execution of the plot. The climax is often more important than the way leading to it − a fact which makes for extreme economy in the development of the plot.

The province of meaning characteristic of the fabliau is reinforced by a particular point of view, which, however, is often hidden coyly behind a serious facade. In no less than two thirds of all the works conventionally classified as fabliaux a lesson is drawn from the tales, in many instances in the form of a moral attached to the end. Also, authors often point to the didactic character of their work. A closer look at these proverbial sayings and morals appended to the tales proves, however, that they are often patently misapplied.[26] The moral tags not only fail to endow the stories with a cloak of decency, but as lessons they are also destroyed by farcial reduction. The lascivious or scatological tale concluded on a pious, sanctimonious note advising the reader to find something useful in the narrative debunks one of the most fundamental medieval literary conventions: that a useful lesson could be drawn from any event. Thus, the moral at its end actually documents the fabliau's unfitness for moralization. In this, the fabliau is diametrically opposed to the exemplum which endeavors to illustrate the validity of a proverbial saying, a doctrine, or an encapsuled norm by means of an exemplary story. In the fabliau, however, the events are removed from this world of ideal conformity and transposed into a world determined by concrete types and situations which refuse resolution through patented moralization. Any serious morals which appear at the end of a fabliau are incongruous. How else could this be in a genre which favors the duper in single action or the dupe turned revenger in multiple action plots? Everything said and done supports his activ-

---

25. See also P. Theiner, "Fabliau Settings", in D. Cooke & B.L. Honeycutt (eds.), *The Humor of the Fabliaux* (Columbia, 1974), pp. 119−36.
26. Cf. the discussions by W.-D. Stempel, "Mittelalterliche Obszönität als literaturästhetisches Problem", in H.R. Jauß (ed.), *Die nicht mehr schönen Künste. Grenzphänomene des Ästhetischen* (München, 1968), p. 198; J. Beyer, pp. 117−57; and N.J. Lacy, "Types of Esthetic Distance in the Fabliaux", in *The Humor of the Fabliaux*, p. 110.

ities and enables him to carry out his deceptive strategies or counterstrategies without incurring punishment. For this reason the authorial point of view in the fabliau is absolutely reliable because the author cannot afford to sacrifice the exigencies of the plot to narrative duplicity. Rather, in maneuvering the characters and shaping the plot, he has to maintain his amoral but biased stance. Thus, whatever he may say on behalf of the dupe is clearly ironic.

By this promotion of the amoral plot structure of his narrative, the fabliau author sets himself apart from the authors of other medieval literary genres. Whereas these tend to support the orthodox world view with its hierarchies, its social norms and moral values, the fabliau author undermines the existing order. By disavowing the metaphysical dimension, the author places man in a different perspective. The fabliaux celebrate the inalienable physicality of man as a selfish, lustful and often animal-like creature who is not to be judged by theological or moral standards. The point of view in the fabliaux is, therefore, not antitheological or antidoctrinal; rather, it is simply elementally human, devoid of any higher ethical aspirations and as such complementary, not opposed, to the view of man as a responsible moral being. The fabliau shows the other side of man and wisely refrains from condemning it.

Point of view and authorial intent have imperceptably merged in the discussion just concluded. They cannot be kept completely separate because both determine one another. The assertion that the point of view governing the fabliau is amoral and dedicated to the presentation of human nature in its full physicality is by necessity also a statement on the author's intent. At least one concept traditionally associated in medieval literature with authorial intent is eliminated thereby: the *docere*. The fabliau does not teach, it entertains.[27] Very appropriately, therefore, Bédier has called the fabliaux "contes a rire",[28] tales designed to produce laughter. Our first impulse as readers will

27. There are numerous statements to this effect made by fabliau authors. Cf. *De la pucele qui abevra le polain, MR*, IV, p. 199, 11. 1–4: "Raconter vueil une aventure / Par joie et par envoiseüre; / Ele n'est pas vilaine à dire, / Mais moz por la gent faire rire." *Dou povre Mercier, MR*, II, p. 114, 11. 4–10: "Se il dit chose qui soit belle, / Elle doit bien estre escoutée; / Car par biaus diz est obliée / Maintes fois ire et cussançons. / Ai abasies granz tançons, / Car, quant aucuns dit les risées, / Les forts tançons sont obliées." *De la Vielle qui oint la palme au chevalier, MR*, V, p. 157, 11. 1–2: "D'une vielle vos voil conter / Une fable por deliter:" *Des .III. Chanoinesses de Couloingne, MR*, III, p. 137, 11. 5–9: "Qui set aucunes truffes dire, / Ou parlé n'ait de duel ne d'ire, / Puis que de mesdit n'i a point, / Maintes foiz vient aussi à point / A l'oïr que fait uns sarmons." *Des trois Avugles de Compiengne, MR*, I, p. 70, 11. 7–9: "Fablel sont bon à escouter: / Maint duel, maint mal font mesconter / Et maint anui et maint meffet."

28. J. Bédier, p. 30.

be to laugh. Yet why do we react that way? What sort of laughter is evoked or provoked by the fabliaux? Is it liberating laughter, or the laughter that sticks in one's throat, or the laughter of embarrassment, or the knowing laughter of those who understand the ways of the world, or the giggle, or the snicker, or the belly laugh? This wide scale of possible sorts of laughter proves that one cannot simply speak of the fabliaux as "contes a rire" without specifying what laughter is meant. This laughter — and we have now reached the point of audience reception — appears to be primarily a laughter at some person or situation. The hearers or readers laugh at some unfortunate dupe who is tricked, at the representative of a certain class whose social pretentiousness or stupidity or lack of manners is ridiculed, at a man or woman who is seduced because of his or her gullibility and innocence. In other words, we normally laugh at the loosers, who do not appeal to our sympathies. Due to the aesthetic distance which keeps the audience from getting involved in the action, no audience identification occurs, not even with the successful protagonist. Consequently, to repeat again, we do not laugh with, but at a character or situation. And the authorial intent is obviously to provoke this kind of laughter which can range from a good natured belly laugh, if human foibles are the author's target, to outright derision. Very seldom do we laugh at witty situations, even though these also exist in some fabliaux where the plot revolves on linguistic ambiguities, a play of metaphors, or the application of a literal interpretation to a symbolic meaning.[29] Disembodied laughter is rare, however, since most of the humor in the fabliaux seems to proceed from man's baser instincts. Still, the laughter thus produced has a consolidating effect on the audience. By laughing at a poor dupe who often belongs to a different social class or estate, the audience may at times feel socially (in general, however, intellectually) superior to him.[30] Of course, the solidarity evoked by the

29. Cf. *De deux Angloys et de l'anel, MR*, II, pp. 178–82 and *De la Male Honte, MR*, V, pp. 95–100 for plots revolving on linguistic ambiguities; *De la Damoisele qui ne pooit oïr parler de foutre, MR*, III, pp. 81–85 and *MR*, V, pp. 24–31, *De la Pucele qui abevra le polain, MR*, IV, pp. 199–207, *De l'Escuiruel, MR*, V, 101–08 and *La Saineresse, MR*, I, pp. 289–93 for a play of metaphors; and *De Brunain, la Vache au prestre, MR*, I, pp. 132–34, *Dou povre Mercier, MR*, II, pp. 114–22 and *De la Vielle qui oint la palme au chevalier, MR*, V, pp. 157–59 for the application of a literal interpretation to a symbolic meaning.
30. Class attribution has been a very thorny problem and a source of great controversy in the study of the fabliaux. We have long departed from Bédier's description of the genre as "poésie ... des carrefours" (p. 371) and from Nykrog's equally limiting assessment of the fabliau as "une sorte de genre courtois" (p. 18). J. Rychner's careful study of several versions of the same story has shown that a reciter could adopt it to make it palatable to different audiences. Moreover, there are many common themes treated in different social milieus, such as the theme of male sexual

fabliaux differs radically from that evoked by the courtly romances, where the audience is asked to share in a system of courtly values. The audience should accept and practice the code of conduct described in these romances — that is, they should identify with the norms presented there — whereas the laughter of the fabliau audience at the misfortune of the dupe is designed to create a distance from the norms and values governing the world of this literary genre.

If one now compares the *Shipman's Tale*, Chaucer's fabliau which supposedly comes closest to the model just devised, with the model itself, one will immediately be struck by the differences noticable in all four structural elements. The communicative situation is constituted by a frame narrative in which personae function as narrators. In this case, moreover, the narrating persona has most likely been changed, since the original teller was probably the Wife of Bath, as indicated by the repeated use of the personal pronoun in the form of the first person plural when the narrator talks about "us women".[31] Also, the catalogue of the virtues good husbands ought to possess, enumerated by the merchant's wife in 11.175–77, is reminiscent of the husbandly ideal propagated by the Wife of Bath in the prologue to her tale. And finally, the role of the wife in the *Shipman's Tale*, deviating from that in any of the known analogues, seems to be more in line with the concept of the wily woman espoused by the Wife of Bath in her prologue than with views the Shipman should hold. From all of this it follows that the substitution of a

ignorance set in a peasant surrounding in *De la Sorisete des estopes*, *MR*, IV, pp. 158–65 and in a courtly environment in *Du sot Chevalier*, *MR*, I, pp. 220–38. The same theme applied to females is set in a noble milieu in *De la Damoisele qui ne pooit oïr parler de foutre*, *MR*, III, pp. 81–85 and in *De la Grue*, *MR*, V, pp. 151 –54, in a bourgeoise milieu in *De l'Escuiruel*, *MR*, V, pp. 101–08, and in a peasant milieu in *De la Damoisele qui n'ot parler de fotre qu'i n'aust mal au cuer*, *MR*, V, pp. 24–31 and in *De la Pucele qui abevra le polain*, *MR*, IV, pp. 199–207. The motif of the woman with two lovers we find with an aristocratic setting in *De l'Espervier*, *MR*, V, pp. 43–51 and with a bourgoise one in *Du Clerc qui fu repus deriere l'escrin*, *MR*, IV, pp. 47–52. And the theme of the husband beaten but content we encounter set in a chivalric milieu in *Romanz de un Chivaler et de sa dame et de un clerk*, *MR*, II, pp. 215–34 and in a bourgoise one in *De la Borgoise d'Orliens*, *MR*, I, pp. 117–25. It may be surmised that the milieu changed to accord or contrast with the audience's expectation of who should be the object of ridicule. Unanimity is only found in the presentation of priests. No matter what the social context may be in which they are placed, they are invariably frustrated and defeated. In other words, the point of view found in the fabliaux and the audience's reaction asked for is strictly anticlerical.

31. *The Canterbury Tales*, VII, ii. 12, 14, and 18. All references are to *The Works of Geoffrey Chaucer*, ed. F.N. Robinson, 2nd ed. (Boston, 1957).

persona as sender for the author/adaptor/performer has a definite influence on the narrative point of view which will inform the *Shipman's Tale*.

In contrast to the world of the fabliau, where social norms and ethical values are frequently lacking, the world of the *Shipman's Tale* is firmly embedded in a fabric of at least secular values. Whether or not these secular virtues are held up as objects of ridicule is a matter of opinion and approach to the tale. If one believes, as Janette Richardson does, that "Chaucer keeps the spiritual ideal in the minds of his audience as a counterbalance to the philosophy of money", one will necessarily arrive at a negative interpretation of the tale's meaning.[32] In such a case all three characters are blind to spiritual reality, a blindness exposed by the author who "transforms an overt fabliau into a moral exemplum".[33] Such a reading, of course, takes the *Shipman's Tale* completely out of the established fabliau context and thus appears to be inimical to the concepts operating in that genre. A more balanced view is provided by V.J. Scattergood, who regards the tale as "Chaucer's most highly developed attempt at defining the nature of the bourgeois mercantile ethos".[34] Scattergood, too, recognizes the limitations inherent in such a world view as espoused by the merchant. His literal-mindedness and his refusal to be deflected from his own sense of things make him vulnerable, but they also give him integrity, and in the final analysis they save him from the knowledge of the deceit practised on him.[35] Scattergood's reading has the great advantage of being, on the one hand, critical of the mercantile value system comprising one aspect of the world presented to us in the *Shipman's Tale* and, on the other hand, reconcilable with the world view informing the fabliau. For the merchant it is a "queynte world" (1.236) – an unsure world, where the chances of success are relatively small. Only two of twelve merchants prosper and live a carefree life up to their old age. Consequently, he is intent on preserving and increasing his material wealth, the very basis of his existence. Since all of his energies are dedicated to the attainment of this goal, "for which (ironically) men helde hym wys" (1.2), he is not cognizant of the existence of other attitudes towards life. His wife and Daun John, however, represent the hedonistic, pleasure oriented world view typical of the fabliau. The merchant's wife only values money for what it can buy, while the monk uses it slyly to obtain

32. J. Richardson, *Blameth Nat Me. A Study of Imagery in Chaucer's Fabliaux* (The Hague, 1970), pp. 118–19.
33. Ibid., pp. 119, 120.
34. V.J. Scattergood, "The Originality of the *Shipman's Tale*", ChauR, 11 (1976/77), 212.
35. Ibid., pp. 225–26.

sexual favors. Money, in short, is for both characters only a means to achieve the end of self gratification, while money for the merchant is his plow which digs the furrow from which more money will grow. Money is thus a means to make more money, which in itself is the sole purpose of money. And in order to reach this goal of monetary increase, the merchant will readily forgo those pleasures deemed so essential by the two other characters. In view of these two diverging attitudes towards material wealth, the conflict already hinted at in the nineteen line introduction is preprogrammed and unavoidable.

With the situation thus arranged, Chaucer could have made use of the typifying characterization ordinarily found in the fabliau, but he departs from the established pattern. Daun John does not conform to the image of the monk, even though this character makes only a rare appearance in the French fabliaux, as in three versions of *Du Segretain ou du moine*.[36] In this story the portrait of the monk corresponds roughly to that of the priest, a decidedly negative figure in the French fabliaux. He is lecherous and willing to buy the love of the lady by giving away possessions belonging to his order.[37] Daun John, too, uses money to ingratiate himself with the members of the merchant's household, but he does so tactfully and it is not clear in the beginning that there may be an ulterior motive for his generosity. In the end he achieves his goal — making love to the merchant's wife — by a ruse, that is, by using the merchant's own plow. His knowledge of the ways of the world, his intellectual astuteness, and his general cleverness, as well as the position he occupies as duper in the affair, are reminiscent of attitudes and roles normally assigned to the clerk in the fabliaux. Instead of being a stereotype of the religious, Daun John is a fairly complex personality when projected against the background of characterization prevalent in the genre of the fabliau.

The merchant, too, in his role as dupe deviates from the type we normally encounter in the fabliaux. For if a merchant there is cast into the role of the dupe he is usually described in negative terms as a greedy usurer.[38] The merchant in the *Shipman's Tale*, however, is a loving husband, a true friend, and

36. *MR*, V, pp. 115–31; *MR*, V, pp. 215–42; *MR*, VI, pp. 117–37.
37. In the French fabliaux the priests seeking sexual favors often offer money to the women they proposition. Cf. *D'Estormi*, *MR*, I, pp. 198–219; *Du Prestre teint*, *MR*, VI, pp. 8–23; *Du Prestre et d'Alison*, *MR*, II, pp. 8–23; and *De Constant du Hamel*, *MR*, IV, pp. 166–98.
38. Cf. *De la Borgoise d'Orliens*, *MR*, I, p. 117, 11. 6–9: "De marchéandise et d'usure / Savoit toz les tors et les poins, / Et ce que il tenoit aus poins / Estoit bien fermement tenu." *De la Dame qui fist hatre son mari*, *MR*, IV, p. 133, 11. 5–7; "Riches hom ert à desmesure; / De marchaandise d'usure / Savoit toz les torz et les poinz;".

a shrewd but honest businessman. He has little in common with the representative of this profession whose ambivalent portrait Chaucer sketches in the *General Prologue*.[39] Trusting in the bonds of friendship, he grants his "deere cosyn" (1.68) John access to his treasure and his wife. His motives are honorable, even though his actions, imprudent within the fabliau context, are bound to invite deception.

That this turn of events will take place, is underscored by the portrayal of the merchant's wife, the character closest to the stereotype of the fabliau. She complains about her husband's sexual neglect and his niggardliness. In order to obtain satisfaction in both areas, she turns to the virile and liberal monk. True to her belief that money is more important than sex, she is primarily interested in obtaining money for the sexual favors she is willing to grant, in order to enable her to pay back the debts she has incurred. After the quick affair with Daun John, she is ready to institute this exchange — sex for money — and make it the basis of her marital relationship with her husband.

With this constellation of characters it is not surprising that deception is the major plot element of the *Shipman's Tale* and in this respect the structure of the tale seems to conform to that of the fabliau. A closer look will demonstrate, however, that the composition of the tale departs from the rule even in regard to this essential structural element. In the two tales most similar to Chaucer's *Shipman's Tale* and also featuring the motif of "the lover's gift regained", Boccaccio's *Decamerone*, VIII,1 and Sercambi's *Novelle*, XIX, the husband plays only a minor part. Although the husband in both analogues is also duped by his wife, who in Boccaccio is greedy and in Sercambi greedy and wanton, the wife herself becomes the real victim of her own deceptive strategies. The development of the plot very clearly aims at this reversal, for it is the woman who has to pay back to her husband the money she believes she earned by granting sexual favors to her lover. The peripety is then followed by the denouement.

In the *Shipman's Tale*, however, the deception is at first solely directed at the merchant. After a long exposition, about half of the tale is given to a detailed account of how Daun John plans to spend a night with the wife of his host. The climax seems to be reached in 11. 313-20, but no peripety takes place. The remainder of the narrative is tripartite: another deception practiced by the wily monk, the climax proper featuring a double peripety, and the denoue-

---

39. See also J. Mann, *Chaucer and Medieval Estate Satire* (Cambridge, 1973), pp. 99–103.

ment. In contrast to the two analogues, where the revelation and resolution occur in the presence of the lover, Daun John is not present at this crucial moment. Rather, he informs the merchant, who visits him on his way to Paris, that he has already repaid the borrowed sum to his wife, thus using the merchant's presence at the convent for a deliberate misinterpretation of the intentions of his visit. During the night of love-making after his return, the merchant confronts his wife with Daun John's statement but the wife is unruffled, turning the seemingly hopeless situation into a victory. Although she does not refrain from cursing this "false monk, daun John" (1. 402) who has put her in an uncomfortable position, she comes up with a plausible explanation and a suggestion of how to repay the debt she owes her husband. The climactic episode of the *Shipman's Tale* is, thus, the pillow talk during which a crisis might have occured if it were not for the wife's presence of mind and the husband's conciliatory attitude. A peripety takes place — the wife is confronted with knowledge that could easily lead to her discomfiture — but this reversal is followed immediately by counterstrategies which cause her husband to experience a change in fortune. He looses a hundred francs, a material loss he can easily sustain because he just earned one thousand francs on his successful business venture.

Fabliau action and mercantile philosophy meet and combine in this decisive scene, a development subtly engineered through the bifocal narrative perspective. The seemingly precise and unambiguous mercantile terms such as "chaffare" "lene", "dettour", "paye" and "taille" are infused with sexual meaning and finally juxtaposed to the merchant's literal understanding of them. Grounded on this ambiguity, a fabliau action can develop running parallel to the business transactions of the merchant. The reader or hearer becomes increasingly aware of the actional potential of these verbal *double entendres*, expecting the fabliau point of view to triumph over the mercantile perspective in order to precipitate the crisis, but such a development fails to materialize. Rather, the two points of view complement and modify one another. Typical of the fabliau version of the tale is a development of the plot featuring the successful deception practiced by the monk and the presence of mind of the merchant's wife in the moment of confrontation. The mercantile spirit, however, infuses the agreement of the couple, an agreement concluded for mutual profit. St. Paul's admonition to observe mutuality in marriage, "Uxori vir debitum reddat similiter autem et uxor viro" (1.Co.7,3), is degraded to the marriage contract, according to which the husband pays for the sexual services of his wife and she can thus buy the apparel necessary for the increase of her husband's honor.[40] Their marriage thereafter will consequently be placed on

40. See also B.S. Levy, "The Quaint World of *The Shipman's Tale*", *SSE*, 4 (1967), 116.

a strictly materialistic basis, a basis, however, promising advantages and satisfaction for both partners. Contrasted with the orthodox view which obviously constitutes the background against which this arrangement is set, this interpretation of the Pauline dictum is as inadequate as its distortion by the Wife of Bath in her prologue. Within the world of the *Shipman's Tale*, though, this solution is fully satisfactory and assured of a smiling acceptance by the audience enjoying the solution of the tale's problematic situation. In recognition of this fact, the narrator can conclude his story within the "pious" wish: "Thus endeth now my tale, and God us sende / Taillynge ynough unto oure lyves ende. Amen." (11.433-34)

The narrator's valediction might be understood as a playful salute to the convention of closing the fabliau with a moral tag. Yet, in a fashion typical of the *Shipman's Tale*, the final distich does not contain the conventional though purposely misapplied moral, but only a double and perhaps even a triple entendre. As homonym the word "taillynge" means "credit" or "sex" and as written pun it can perhaps also mean "tales".[41] In any case, there can be no doubt that the homonymic pun is intentional, as is indicated by the wife's frivolous offer to her husband in 11.414-24 to reimburse him in bed for the one hundred francs spent on clothes. At the end of the *Shipman's Tale*, therefore, the playful element becomes increasingly more important, an element which gains momentum throughout the tale. The action narrated under these circumstances thus reaches a new level which is obviously located above the narrow confines of the mercantile world on the one hand and the world of the fabliau on the other. Both world views are resolved in a joke and thus lose their originally postulated validity.

Consequently, the reaction to the *Shipman's Tale* is neither derision nor laughter at anyone. All characters, even the merchant, retain their unviolated identity. In this, his fate differs greatly from that of the other dupes in Chaucer's fabliaux, like the carpenter John in the *Miller's Tale*, the miller Symkyn in the *Reeve's Tale* and January in the *Merchant's Tale*, who all become objects of ridicule. No one is ridiculed in the *Shipman's Tale*; rather, the laughter provoked by this tale is directed at the comic situation arising from the combination by means of verbal manipulation of two mutually exclusive world views. Instead of distancing laughter at the deserved fate of the dupes, our reaction will be a bemused smile at the humorous *concordia discors* achieved through *double entendres*.

41. Cf. especially the discussion by G. Joseph, "Chaucer's Coinnage: Foreign Exchange and the Puns of the *Shipman's Tale*", *ChauR*, 17 (1982/83), 349–50; 254–55.

The Reeve's Tale

Derek Brewer

I

The Reeve's Tale concerns a proud, bullying miller at Trumpington near
Cambridge and his equally proud wife. They have a daughter aged 20, of
lusty attractiveness, and also, rather improbably, a baby six months old.
Millers were traditionally regarded as both prosperous and thievish. They
were important but not very popular members of the community. This
miller has a contract to grind the corn for a college in Cambridge called
The King's Hall. The Manciple, i.e. manager, of this Hall has fallen sick, and
so two of the students decide that they will take the grain to the miller and
supervise its grinding in order to prevent theft. They are bumptious, patron-
ising young men and the miller easily tricks them by releasing their horse,
which runs off into the fen and keeps them chasing it all day. The miller
meanwhile grinds their corn and steals some of it. The two young men catch
the horse in the end but find that it is too late to get back into college, because of the curfew. They therefore ask the miller to put them up for the
night. The miller has only one bedroom with three beds in it. He and his wife
sleep in one bed with the baby's cradle at the foot of it, his daughter sleeps in
another and the two young men are put in the third. They have a jolly supper
at the students' expense, and go to bed. During the night one of the young
men gets into bed with the miller's daughter. The other one lies awake feeling
very sorry for himself and thinking what a spineless fool he will appear when
the story is told. However, the miller's wife has to get up to answer the call of
nature and when she does so the young man moves the cradle from the foot
of her bed to the foot of his. When she returns she goes to her own bed but
misses the cradle, and since everywhere is very dark, thinks she has mistaken
her way. So in all innocence she gets into the student's bed, where she receives
a warm welcome. As the night draws on the other student, who had been
with the daughter, decides to get back with his friend. He goes to his own
bed, but finds the cradle at the foot of it. He makes a mistake similar to that
of the wife's, thinks he has gone to the wrong bed, and so gets into bed with
the miller. Thinking the miller is the other student, he wakes him up and

tells him what he has done. The miller is outraged and they fight each other. The noise wakes the wife who thinks that the two students are fighting. She gets up, finds a stick by the wall, and brings it down with a fearful crack on the bald head of her own husband. The students take advantage of this to beat him further, then dress, take their horse and their ground meal and depart. To crown all, the miller's daughter gives them the product of the stolen wheat in the form of a large baked loaf.

The story is told with wonderfully realistic, vivid detail of many kinds. The details about the students who come from King's Hall are fully authentic.[1] It sounds a genuine anecdote of Cambridge student life.

II

In fact, the story is not original. The earliest version of it is a French fabliau of 1190–94. There is another French version of the thirteenth century. There are two thirteenth-century German versions, a version by Boccaccio in the *Decameron* written between 1349 and 1353, and there is a whole series of later versions in various languages.[2] In other words, it is a traditional story, an example of the International Popular Medieval Comic Tale.

Traditional literature is of its nature rather different from the kind we have become accustomed to since the seventeenth century in Europe and America. It is influenced by and illustrates characteristics derived from 'oral literature' even though it is written; its identity is fluid, being capable of many variants in differing versions; the story may 'grow'; the action is more fundamental than the characters; the tale itself has a certain independence of the teller and the setting of any particular version, and imposes certain constraints about them, yet any version itself is also adapted by particular tellers to suit particular settings. There are other characteristics which differentiate traditional literature from modern Western literature; it is more patterned; it rests on mental structures, and realism is secondary; suspense is less important than fulfilment; irony is less pervasive; style more transparent, and so forth. What I wish to emphasise at this point, however, is the unquestionable fact that our present-day normal assumptions, expectations and even literary theories un-

1. D. Brewer, "*The Reeve's Tale* and the King's Hall, Cambridge", in *Tradition and Innovation in Chaucer* (London, 1982), pp. 73–9 and J.A.W. Bennett, *Chaucer at Oxford and Cambridge* (Oxford 1974).
2. L.D. Benson, and T.M. Andersson, *The Literary Context of Chaucer's Fabliaux* (Indianapolis 1971).

less they are adjusted are the product of *modern* literature. If we do not adjust them we may well misunderstand, even if we enjoy traditional literature. *The Reeve's Tale*, like much other medieval literature has often suffered from misunderstandings induced by implicit reference to modern conceptions. The present essay approaches *The Reeve's Tale* specifically as an example of traditional literature to show it in a new light.

A traditional story is often most fruitfully approached by modern critics in relation to its analogues. Knowledge of the analogues creates, for the modern critic, a situation analogous so that of the traditional reader or hearer of a story or song. A traditional story is likely to be known in outline, if only vaguely, to at least some of the hearers or readers of any particular version. They, and the author of that particular version, will have certain expectations in common, will unconsciously recognise certain constants which make it *that* story and not another, yet will also recognise and enjoy novel variants of many kinds, both in structure and detail. Since it is not practicable here to compare all the variants of *The Reeve's Tale* the two German versions will be used as the chief examples.

III

Germany is particularly rich in examples of the International Medieval Comic Tale. There are about two hundred, written down from the early thirteenth to the sixteenth centuries. The German versions of *The Reeve's Tale* are *Das Studentenabenteuer* and *Irregang und Girregar*. They seem to have been composed in ignorance of each other and have a number of interesting differences. However, they are sufficiently similar to be discussed together. The tale is told entirely from the point of view of the youths, as is the case with all the versions except Chaucer's. The youths are students, as they are in all versions of the story except Boccaccio's. They are travelling in order to study, in one case at the University of Paris. They are rich and cheerful. On their journey they pass through a town and one of them takes a great fancy to a pretty girl whom he sees. They decide to ask the father for lodging in his house, and although in one version the father agrees readily and in the other he is reluctant, there is little difficulty. In each case the young men provide food and drink, and the one who is in love with the daughter makes advances to her. There is little discussion of the arrangements of the house but there is some crowding, and in each case the one in love makes his way secretly and successfully to the daughter's bed. Then, of course, his friend is disconsolate. The wife gets up to go outside and so the second student moves the cradle in order to mislead her, and succeeds in getting her into his bed. Then comes the climax when the first student leaves the girl, lies down with the host, and boasts of his adventure. A fight follows. In *Das Studentenabenteuer* the wife eventually brings a light and the second student succeeds in getting the first student back into his own bed where they both pretend to be asleep. The wife, well aware of what has happened and wishing to conceal it, persuades the husband that he has made a mistake and advises him to say nothing. The two students then leave cheerfully the next morning. In *Irregang und Girregar* the wife more elaborately persuades her husband that he has had a nightmare, and the students read a mock prayer over him. There is then a long and extraordinary continuation in which the two young men continue to stay in the house for several days and play rough tricks of a folkloric kind on the host, so that he thinks he is mad, while the two young men continue to make love to both his wife and his daughter. This second part is a brutal and unique elaboration of the traditional tale, much less courtly than the first part, but apparently by the same author. Such individual variants are characteristic of traditional narrative. Their presence does not alter the fact that we are dealing with the same story.

IV

Recognition of the existence of variants, each with its own validity, of the same story, leads to several important points.

First, in traditional literature, the framework, or structure, or leading elements, or nucleus of events, however, one likes to call it, even if that itself varies somewhat in each version, is the distinguishing factor, known by its pattern or 'shape', which makes the story in question *that* story and not another story. This pattern is independent of any particular version, though it can only be known through one or more actual versions. It may be thought of as 'pre-verbal', even though in the nature of the case only to be described in words, which will themselves constitute a version, which will not have absolute authority over other versions. The pre-verbal pattern will be a recognisable, not totally variable, but not totally fixed, cluster of motifs, more or less elaborate. Some of the grandest and most fruitful stories have a very simple pattern at their heart, like the Arthurian story, at whose centre lies the simple sequence, 'the great king dies'. Other stories have more precise and elaborate patterns, and such is the case with the story which we know in Chaucer's work as

The Reeve's Tale, of which the variant versions have a closely similar structure. Whether simple or elaborate, the story-pattern is the distinguishing, fundamental characteristic.

The second point is that the different versions of the same tale may imply different attitudes, describe different settings, employ different kinds of character, and attribute different motives to characters. General attitudes and purposes with which the story is told may vary.

Thirdly, character and characterisation are therefore secondary to the fundamental pattern and action of the story, which are already determined. (By 'character' I mean the appearance, nature and motives attributed to the agents of the story: by 'characterisation' I mean the *way* in which a particular agent is described by the teller of a given version, fully or briefly, externally or internally, with sympathy or hostility.) All these may vary in different versions of the same story.

We tend to think, because we are accustomed to reading novels, and the accounts by novelists telling us how they write what they claim are original, not traditional stories, that the relationship between character and event is causal. The author thinks of a character and then allows him or her to act — "what will she do?" asks Henry James of his own imaginative creation.[3] The character acts, produces results which have further consequences, and so a chain of cause and effect is established. Modern novelists as different as Dickens, Henry James and Graham Greene have testified that a character takes on 'a life of his own', as it were independent of the author, who then follows the character's actions with interest and even surprise, to discover what will be done, what will be felt. The novelist analyses the fictional character and will know more about his inner life than might be the case in 'real life', but the modern novelist often thinks of himself or herself as an historian following a unique, independent person and recording specific actions and individual responses. Thus in modern literature the character is primary and unique, initiating actions of which the outcome is, at least theoretically, at first unknown even to the author. (This is only in reality part of the full psychological and literary truth, but it is generally accepted by modern writers and readers. Naturally there is nothing objectionable in it, but it is very different from the way traditional literature works upon us.)

---

3. H. James, *The Art of the Novel* (New York, 1907). The phrase comes from the Preface to *The Portrait of a Lady*, all of which is relevant to the present discussion.

In traditional literature, by contrast, the pattern of events precedes the character. The kind of question a traditional storyteller might ask himself or herself is not 'What will the character do?' but, 'How shall I present these events?', 'How shall I make them convincing?', or 'What kind of a character would do such things?'. More subtle questions were no doubt put or felt by Chaucer, but the whole approach of storyteller and reader (or hearer) is different because they already know, or will recognise the basic material or general substance of the story.

We may thus describe the nature of a traditional story in terms of its substance and its accidents. The substance is the recognisable cluster or shapes of events, recognised as a whole pattern, not discovered as a new sequence, and recognised continually by different people at different times and places. The accidents are the characters, characterisations, points of view, language, descriptions, dialogues, etc. etc. through which the substance is realised. The analogy of substance and accident is crude and only temporary, without valuejudgements made or implied, but useful for a moment to enable us to focus on that elusive central pattern which enables us to recognise what is substantially the same story in many different guises, with many different accidents.

The substance is best seen as pattern or shape, and we begin with it because that is where the identity and the fundamental general appeal of the story must lie, however, modified in specific versions.

V

The pattern of the story of *The Reeve's Tale* when most generally expressed shows the victory of the young over the old. More specifically it illustrates the aggressiveness of young men towards the established order of possession and protection, authority and convention. Aggression is focussed especially on sexual desire, but also though secondarily on wealth. The father-victim has to be well-off, though the aggressors are not poor. Accompanying sexual aggression by young men, according to the story-pattern, are the concepts that women, old or young, are accomplices rather than objects or victims, and old men are fools.

When the pattern of the story is thus rendered in general abstract terms it sounds not only true and sympathetic to many common attitudes but also platitudinous. The obviousness is part of the attraction of the story, since it is embodied in an interesting sequence of events. To put it another way, the story incarnates in an interesting manner accepted truths; the truth may well be only subconsciously or subliminally recognised but it is important because it represents the story's depth and truth to life. However fantastic a story may be, it has to embody some truth to life for it to be valued and repeated.

This particular pattern if sufficiently generally expressed might seem to be capable of being told in either a tragic or a comic manner, if for example the victim were presented with pathos. That would not accord with traditional attitudes. I have argued elsewhere that the inherent nature of tragedy, at least when conflict between generations is, as so often, the subject, requires that parents in some way destroy the children. When the children destroy the parents (metaphorically, of course) the result is invariably comedy − or romance.[4] That must obviously be the case for biological reasons, for the very continuation of the race. That is why we are always, willy-nilly, on the side of the young. In *The Reeve's Tale* the young are the children, the father is, of course, the father. Hence the story of *The Reeve's Tale* can only lend itself properly to comic treatment, and has only ever done so. In the most general terms this story is about killing the father, winning the mother, and getting away with it, as everyone wants to do.

The comedy, like most comedy, is based on reversal, and incongruity; authority and respectability are made fools of, unscrupulous rascals are successful, and win both the money and the women. Since we identify with the young rascals we are not unduly upset. On the other hand, we also, if we have any sense of order, sympathise with decency, respectability and authority. It is only because of this dual sympathy that we can appreciate the incongruity and contradiction embodied in the reversal of morality which makes us laugh.

Once again we recognise that these cool intellectual abstractions in themselves do not make us laugh. We are not laughing but examining why we laugh. The analysis presupposes that we have laughed with and enjoyed the works of art which embody the abstractions in lively, imaginable fashion. The structures pointed to by the abstractions are really there, and so are our responses. The aim of analysis is to understand how and why they work, not to offer a substitute for the artistic experience. But recognition of the nature of the underlying abstractions increases our understanding of this and other stories.

The pattern of the story in *The Reeve's Tale* has some interesting similarities to and differences from those of the so-called fairy-tale. Fairy-tales, to put it

4. D. Brewer, *Symbolic Stories* (Cambridge 1980).

with crude brevity in abstract terms, are about growing up, getting rid of our parents, winning our beloved. The process usually includes reconciliation with parent-figures and other elements such as separation from and final integration with society, usually in the form of isolation followed by marriage. Fairy-tales are more interested in love than sex, and are more universal in implication than the story in *The Reeve's Tale*, partly because the protagonist may be either female or male. The story in *The Reeve's Tale* is defined by the fact that it must be about young men; there is no reconciliation with the father-figure; if the wife is a mother-figure then she is won in rivalry with the father-figure in order to be abandoned; and the young men simply go away. The story has less universal application then a fairy-tale, which does not make it less entertaining, even if it is less profound.

The essential pattern of the story, like that of so many International Medieval Popular Comic Tales, implies no concern with justice, decency, honesty or generosity. The husband's trust and hospitality are shamefully betrayed, and even his wife and daughter collude with the young betrayers. All one can say here is that life is all too often like that. Perhaps it is the nature of life that the young shall betray and treat with ingratitude the old, and we had better laugh (especially when old) in order not to cry. We shall notice, however, that Chaucer modifies the cruel pattern of the comedy of Nature.

Leaving aside such moral considerations we may notice how aesthetically pleasing is the ingenuity of cross-patterning in the structure of the story. The seduction of the daughter is paralleled by the cunning ingenuity of the seduction of her mother, but the simplicity of the daughter's seduction is matched by the simple-minded boasting of her seducer, not to the apparently simple other student, but to the father himself. Sex with the mother is paralleled and contrasted with boasting to the father, which involves the further comedy of conflict between husband and wife. We shall notice again how Chaucer enriches this theme in his own version by positing affection between husband and wife, which makes their inadvertent conflict the more comic, but also, because of the way he characterises both, less unfair. In many versions the father/husband remains in ignorance of what has happened, but Chaucer again realises the aesthetic pattern most fully by producing a full recognition by everyone of what has happened, a comic *anagnorisis*, a conscious awareness that is deeply satisfying.

VI

A storyteller takes a traditional tale and re-tells it to an audience who know, or sense, the basic pattern, and then he tells it in his own version, with his own particular interests. We learn a good deal both from the nature of the story he selects, and the variations he employs when he re-tells it.

Why did Chaucer take this particular story? We obviously cannot ask the question in ordinary practical terms but it is legitimate to deduce, from the artistic quality of *The Reeve's Tale*, and its variations from the analogues, what is the purport of the story as he tells it; what Chaucer is in general saying to us. By asking questions we may enhance our understanding and enjoyment.

We must first take into account the developing drama of *The Canterbury Tales*.[5] Chaucer at this point must have felt he needed another comic tale to correspond with *The Miller's Tale*. (Correspondence, parallelism, rather than causation, characterise traditional narrative.) He had written *The General Prologue* with a variety of characters including a Miller and Reeve and he had had the marvellous and original idea of allowing the characters to interact independently amongst themselves. In this respect he is extraordinarily modern and approaches more nearly than any other English writer before the seventeenth century to the conception of autonomous characters. It is as if he follows their actions as does the modern novelist. He had discovered a quarrel between the Reeve and the Miller. The basis of this is undoubtedly traditional. The Reeve was the farm manager and his natural enemy would have been the Miller, who was independent of him but with whom he had to deal. So reeves and millers would not be expected to get on. He had made the Reeve also a choleric man and one therefore who, since he had been a carpenter himself, objected to the victim of *The Miller's Tale* being represented as a carpenter. So Chaucer needed to find a story which would suit his dramatic plan of giving the Reeve something to say which could be a counterblast to the mockery of a carpenter in *The Miller's Tale*. We may then imagine Chaucer sorting through the variety of folktales which he had heard to think of one which would be a suitable vehicle for the kind of thing he had in mind. What sort of tale could the Reeve tell? It will be recalled that *The Miller's Tale* is another International Medieval Comic Popular Tale with numerous analogues which Chaucer made much more ingenious and rich. He wanted a comic

5. D. Brewer, *Introduction to Chaucer* (London 1984).

tale of a similar kind which he could use as a counter-weight to *The Miller's Tale*. He needed a tale which would mock and make a butt of a miller. No other version of *The Reeve's Tale* makes the husband a miller but it is of the essence of the story that it is about a properous householder who is betrayed and beaten in his own house. The tale makes a butt of the householder. It is also notable that in most versions of the story those who trick the house-holder are students. Chaucer was interested in Oxford and Cambridge.[6] He knew both universities and though his closest associations were with Oxford, parliament had been held in Cambridge and he knew some Cambridge men. He also knew East Anglia well, and Cambridge University had a number of East Anglian associations for obvious reasons. The Reeve himself comes from Norfolk, which is an area from which Cambridge drew a number of students. The combination of students and a householder in the story which would be balanced against an Oxford story pointed to a Cambridge setting. Chaucer knew the King's Hall Cambridge and may well have had friends there or, perhaps, enemies. He had to find a reason for the students to visit the house where they were to play their tricks. It was here that the traditional hostility between reeve and miller may have suggested that the householder should be a miller. No doubt all these ideas came together much less analytically than I have suggested.

Whether or not this reconstruction be true can never be proved, but what is incontrovertible is that Chaucer, while not changing the general structure of the story, gives it a slant different from all the other versions, and this change depends on his perception, or his artistic need, of the householder as the butt and thus the centre of the story. All the other stories centre on the students. Their motive is provided by the desire of one of them for the girl. (In terms of the analysis of folktale they provide an interesting example of the 'split hero'. Psychologically the two are one.[7] The very modernity of Chaucer's sense of character is built upon the traditional methods of narrative. He 'adds' motivation to, and changes motivation in, a given structure of events. To sum-marise, he has a particular kind of butt in mind and needs a set of actions to ridicule him; finding a set of actions which can be used to mock a butt he then supplies characters and motivations to make the actions interesting and plausible. He takes pleasure in the pattern of actions which tradition supplies in a particular tale, then links them in such a way as to supply a sense of cau-sality.

6. D. Brewer, *Chaucer and his World* (London 1977) and J.A.W. Bennett, *op. cit.*, n. 1.
7. D. Brewer, "The Poetry of Chaucer's Fabliaux", in *Chaucer: the Poet as Storyteller* (London 1984), pp. 107–19.

He begins his story then, not with the students, as other versions do, but with the characterisation of the miller of Trumpington and his wife – a rich piece of description too long and too well-known to be quoted here. This description is not, however, the exploratory autonomous characterisation of the modern novelist but the traditional characterisation of a type. The miller is a bully, greedily possessive both of goods and family, arrogant and dishonest. For good measure Chaucer builds in an ill-founded social pride. Chaucer is writing for courtiers and he appeals to the amusement of a superior social class contemplating the absurd pretentiousness of a low-class character priding himself on a wife who herself is pert and proud because she is the illegitimate daughter of a priest, and has brought a good dowry with her of 'many a pan of brass'. All this, though snobbish in a way, is not cruel. Chaucer's characterisation, it should be noted, is 'moral' in the old sense – not moralistic, but (I quote the OED) "pertaining to character or disposition considered as good or bad, virtuous or vicious; of or pertaining to the distinction between right and wrong, or good and evil, in relation to the actions, volitions or character of responsible beings". The field of action is social and everyday, deliberately not profound. The character is fully formed, not psychologically structured; static, not capable of development. The action of the story will not change the character of the miller or of any one else.

This characterisation is moral also because through it he creates a reason for the action different from that in the analogues. This has considerable implications. The two clerks go to the mill at Trumpington because of the miller's dishonesty and merely to protect the interests of their college. It is only after they have been cheated and humiliated that they exact a punishment which if it does not exactly suit the crime is in a sense justified by it, is connected with it. We feel that it is peculiarly suited to the character of the miller, though the truth must be, since we know that the action precedes the character, that in fact the character has been made 'suitable' to the action. A proud dishonest bully is hurt in pride, and deprived of the fruits of his dishonesty, because to make him a dishonest bully is the only way that the events can be decently enjoyed. Unconstrained sexuality is the instrument, not, as in the analogues, the deplorable, if natural, motive. The structure of reason and morality which Chaucer creates implies that the underlying basis of life is rational, humane and moral. Sexual appetite, opportunism, violence are involved. The roughness of life is not sentimentalised, and the reversals of fortune are hugely comic, but they are not totally arbitrary. Though material reality is powerful, and may call into ridicule human pretentiousness, material reality is also related to moral decency. If the miller had been honest, Chaucer makes us feel, he would not have suffered as he did.

78

The structure of the story thus in Chaucer's rendering becomes itself not only aesthetically but also morally pleasing. The aesthetic pattern is the more fundamental, being found in the analogues, but the rationalisation which Chaucer creates within the structure, by centering it on the miller, the butt, rather than on the commonplace motivation in the analogues of immoral youthful animal desire, creates a moral and social dimension which is itself poetic. Poetry resides in units larger than words alone, though those units are created through words. The pattern is at once aesthetic, moral and social, created by the concept of a rationally connected physical universe which is related to human aesthetic pleasure in correspondences. This pleasure is paralleled by moral pleasure in the humane value of social justice. All this is achieved in *The Reeve's Tale* without the faintest trace of moralisation, didacticism or allegory.

VII

It is not surprising that the educated mind is presented in this poem as superior. The educated mind of the storyteller, implicit in the narrative of actions and descriptions, is barely apparent in the analogues, even in Boccaccio's version.

In responding to the educated nature of the narration we respond to much on the surface (not in any trivialising sense the superficial elements) of the style and the storyteller's, i.e. Chaucer's, attitude. Chaucer's strong sense of the difference between educated and uneducated men is clear from the preceding *Miller's Tale*, as well as elsewhere in *The Canterbury Tales*. In *The Reeve's Tale* the difference is made plain in the passage where the miller is persuaded to offer overnight accommodation to the two clerks. He says derisively

> ..., "If ther be eny,
> Swich as it is, yet shal ye have youre part.
> Myn hous is streit, but ye han lerned art;
> Ye konne by argumentes make a place
> A myle brood of twenty foot of space.
> Lat se now if this place may suffise,
> Or make it rowm with speche, as is youre gise."
> (I, 4120-4126)

The miller is a plain sensible man and thinks that all intellectuals are silly, as most plain men do. Dislike of education is rather characteristic of the English lower classes (unlike the Welsh or Scots), perhaps because since the Norman

Conquest education has seemed often to come in an alien language from a superior alien class. The miller's jest is in itself quite a good one, relating to discussions of the power of the mind, and of course totally unrealistic in formulation – no uneducated miller could speak so – though realistic in its expression of a typical plain-man's attitude. There is no doubt that the miller and his family are of lower class and education than Chaucer's audience. The miller's daughter uses such words as *lemman* 'sweetheart', unquestionably provincial, low-class and uneducated in Chaucer's stylistic register. The two clerks are by definition well educated and though they are young they must have been, in the peculiar structure of the King's Hall, Fellows, i.e. full members of the corporation. They would have had courtly connections to get there and men from King's Hall often proceeded to be courtiers and clerics in the King's court. They speak in a northern accent which for some reason always seems comical to southerners, but this is in a period before regional dialects are associated with inferior class-status or inferior education. The derision of the miller for educated men, like the similar derision of the carpenter in *The Miller's Tale*, is shown to be ill-founded. Education for Chaucer indicates superior brain-power, persistence, ingenuity and success.

VIII

Education, rationality and causality come together in the realism with which *The Reeve's Tale* is told. Mind may ultimately control matter, but matter is very important.

Chaucer's version is much more realistic, in the sense of rendering physical circumstance more vivid and plausible, than any of the analogues. It is really quite remarkable how sharply Chaucer realises for us the particular dimensions of the house and the arrangement of the bedroom. As he developed as a poet he was more and more attracted towards the description of ordinary plausible physical reality, and this tendency in him is a modernistic one which found its fullest fruition centuries later in the novel. Lively representation of appearances and actions is not all. Chaucer outdoes himself in the way that he links actions, objects and motives together in a strong chain of cause and effect. Since we know that the story existed before, we can say with some certainty that since it is intrinsically a fantasy any strong sense of plausible material cause and effect must be imposed upon it by the author of that particular version. Chaucer is quite outstanding in the way he connects the various items of the action together and connects the actions to the characters. To give a small example, the miller's bald head is emphasised in the elaborate description of him at the beginning of the tale. At that point such a vivid detail may seem merely to reflect the arbitrariness of perception which contributes to the impression of reality. This detail appears in no analogue. As it turns out it is part of the chain of cause and effect. At the farcical climax of the tale with the fight in the bedroom the wife tries to help her husband by hitting one of the students on the head with a staff. She sees something white glimmering in the dark, and thinks that one of the students must be wearing a white night-cap. (Chaucer incidentally appears to be the first English writer to refer in English to night-caps.) But the white thing is of course her husband's bald head on which she smartly brings down her staff. A trail of powder is laid at the very beginning of the story which explodes the powder-keg at the end.

The astonishing realism of the poem and the way in which concrete facts are connected together by cause and effect are seen most vividly in the passage about the fight. It is a wonderfully solid piece of narration, which I have analysed in detail elsewhere.[8]

> This John stirte up as faste as ever he myghte,
> And graspeth by the walles to and fro,
> To fynde a staf; and she stirte up also,
> And knew the estres bet than dide this John,
> And by the wal a staf she foond anon,
> And saugh a litel shymeryng of a light,
> For at an hole in shoon the moone bright;
> And by that light she saugh hem bothe two,
> But sikerly she nyste who was who,
> But as she saugh a whit thyng in hir ye.
> And whan she gan this white thyng espye,
> She wende the clerk hadde wered a volupeer,
> And with the staf she drow ay neer and neer,
> And wende han hit this Aleyn at the fulle,
> And smoot the millere on the pyled skulle,
> That doun he gooth, and cride, "Harrow! I dye!"
> Thise clerkes beete hym weel and lete hym lye;
> And greythen hem, and took hir hors anon,
> And eek hire mele, and on hir wey they gon.
> And at the mille yet they tooke hir cake
> Of half a busshel flour, ful wel ybake.
> (I, 4292-4312)

---

8. Ibid., p. 76.

IX

The Reeve's Tale would sustain a good deal more detailed analysis than is possible here. The style is full-Chaucerian, varied, often concrete, sententious, but not in any dramatic sense characteristic of the Reeve himself. Although the Northern dialect of the clerks bears some relationship to the dialect of Norfolk (from which the Reeve is said to come) the rest of the poem is entirely free from such dialectal characteristics. That is why the clerks' speech stands out so comically. So there is no attempt to make *The Reeve's Tale* in any sense a dramatic monologue.

Nor is there any so-called Narrator, different from the poet-as-storyteller. The presence of a Narrator must always imply a self-conscious irony indicated within the text. There is no evidence of irony of this kind in *The Reeve's Tale* (indeed there is far less evidence for it in most of Chaucer's poetry than most modern critics seem to believe). The general structure of the story is adapted to suit the general dramatic situation of the Reeve's quarrel with the pilgrim-Miller. But Chaucer attempts no further detailed characterisation. He took a traditional International Comic Tale and adapted and enriched it in a variety of ways. He placed it in a dramatic situation, connected the actions, re-orientated and deepened the moral implications of the structure, gave it a social dimension, created characters to fit the actions, enriched the style of actual narration. All this is done in the service of social and moral comedy based on the simple but profound observation that 'pride goes before a fall', and the biter may be bit. Physical circumstance brings down undue spiritual assertion. Chaucer draws the picture, tells the story, with his inimitable human detachment, superiority combined with sympathy, derision with toleration. His Christian humanism is fully aware of the wickednesses and absurdities of the world; his morality takes fully into account the nature of brute matter; his standards are implied without any recourse to preaching or moralising; his philosophy fully recognises the possibilities of betrayal and defeat; and in the end cheerfulness will insist on breaking in.

His desir wol fle withouten wynges:

Mary and Love in Fourteenth-Century Poetry

Piero Boitani

The medieval history of Marian devotion and theology is long and complex. Similarly varied and fascinating is the development that the figure of the Virgin undergoes in the visual arts. And a particularly important place is occupied in medieval devotional poetry by the eulogies of, and the prayers to, the Virgin, the forms of which were described thirty-five years ago by Erich Auerbach in a memorable article.[1]

The scope of the present essay is more limited. Its purpose is to examine the versions of Marian prayers left to us in lyrical and narrative poetry by four great fourteenth-century writers – Dante, Guillaume de Deguileville, Petrarch, and Chaucer. The reasons for doing this are fundamentally three. In the first place, all four poets use prayers to the Virgin at crucial moments of their works. Secondly, the prayers by Dante and Deguileville directly influenced Chaucer. Thirdly, a comparative study of their contexts may tell us something about fourteenth-century changes in religious attitudes and above all about personal and narrative strategies, throwing some light on Chaucer's technique in the *Troilus* and the *Canterbury Tales*.

The first stage of our story begins with Dante,[2] whose decision to make St Bernard invoke the Virgin in Canto XXXIII of *Paradiso* just before the poet-protagonist has the ultimate vision of God, responds to a precise poetic and religious logic. While contemplating the mystical rose and the "general form of Paradise" in Canto XXXI Dante, it will be remembered, turns around to ask Beatrice some questions as to which his mind is "in suspense" (55–7). To his great surprise, instead of seeing Beatrice, he finds before him an old man, "clad like the folk in glory". He immediately asks him, "Ov'è ella?", where is she (64). And the "tender father", whose eyes and cheeks are "suffused with

1. E. Auerbach, "Dante's Prayer to the Virgin (*Par.* XXXIII) and Earlier Eulogies", *Romance Philology*, III (1949), 1–26.
2. The edition of Dante's *Comedy* used here is that of G. Petrocchi (Turin, 1975). The translations are taken from C. Singleton's edition (1970–75).

benign gladness" (61–2), replies that Beatrice has urged him from his place to fulfill Dante's desire. She is now in her throne, "in the circle which is third from the highest tier" (65–9), and Dante, without answering the old man, lifts up his eyes to behold his lady making a crown for herself as she reflects the eternal rays of God's light (70–2). The distance between the poet and Beatrice is infinite, but this makes no difference to Dante, for her image comes down unblurred by aught between (76–8). Dante fervently thanks her aloud for having saved and freed him, and prays her to now loose his soul from his body (79–80). Distant as she seems, Beatrice smiles and looks on him and then turns again to the "eternal fountain" (91–3). The holy elder who accompanies him invites the poet to fly with his eyes throughout the "garden" of the Empyrean, and declares that the Queen of Heaven, for whom he himself is all afire with love, will grant them every grace, "però ch'i' sono il suo fedel Bernardo", since he is her faithful Bernard (94–102).

The recognition scene that follows, the last human anagnorisis of the poem, fuses earthly and heavenly in an extraordinary, and peculiarly Dantean, amalgam. What Dante experiences when the old man reveals himself as St Bernard of Clairvaux at the very summit of Paradise is compared to the emotion felt by a pilgrim who comes to Rome from, say, Croatia to look at the 'Veronica', i.e., the true image ('vera icona') of Jesus' visage imprinted on a veil which a woman handed him to wipe the sweat off his face while he climbed the Calvary — a cloth that was exhibited in St Peter's every year. Like this foreign pilgrim, whose "old hunger" for the icon is not sated but who, when the relic is shown, exclaims in his thought, 'My Lord Jesus Christ, true God, was then your semblance like to this?', Dante gazes on the "living charity" of him who "in questo mondo, contemplando, gustò di quella pace". Aware of the poet's intense scrutiny, Bernard interrupts this rapture with an exquisitely gentle, slightly jocose comment: My dear son, you cannot contemplate Heaven if you keep your eyes only down here at the bottom of it! Look up instead until you see "the Queen to whom this realm is subject and devoted" (103–17).

Dante's 'hic et nunc', the specific moment of his journey when he recognizes St Bernard acquires in this passage a threefold historical dimension and prefigures the supreme stage of his beatific vision. Concentrated in three *terzine*, we have a vivid image of contemporary life — the pilgrim from Croatia looking at Veronica's veil — which sends us back to Christ's earthly features and simultaneously to the Saint who, *in this world*, tasted of that 'peace' (the ultimate bliss of Heaven) through contemplation. Dante's recognition of Bernard is like the pilgrim's recognition of Jesus' visage on the Veronica. But Dante himself, the spiritual pilgrim of the other world, will soon recognize "our effigy", the image of the Son of Man, in God's essence (XXXIII, 127–32). Dante, who is entering the very last stage of his beatific vision, will soon fulfill within himself the 'taste' Bernard had of that peace in his mystical experiences on earth. In his surprise, moreover, the Croatian pilgrim expresses the unsoundable depth of the mystery of the Incarnation that Dante will try to describe in Canto XXXIII. In his thoughts, the historical, human 'semblance' of Jesus is superimposed onto the idea of the 'Lord' and the 'Dio verace'.

The complex presence in this passage of both projection of the earthly onto the eternal and reflection of the eternal into the earthly should not make us forget that this interplay is in a sense incidental – that in fact what Dante is describing is the climax of the surprise he felt when, instead of Beatrice, he found the old man at his side, and the wonder he now feels as a lifelong expectation (the "antica fame")is finally fulfilled by the recognition of the old man as Bernard of Clairvaux, the great saint of the twelfth century. This is a strong human emotion, heightened by the peculiar awareness of an intellectual who has studied Bernard's works and knows (and celebrates, by presenting him here) their importance for the culture of his world and for him personally – an emotion similar to that Dante experienced when he found his first guide, Virgil, in the dark wood.

Like Virgil, Bernard is 'moved' to Dante's help by Beatrice, and becomes the poet's last guide. His function is precisely that of directing Dante's heart and mind towards Mary, the intermediary *par excellence* between man and God, that through her he may come closer to the Supreme Being and that she may obtain for him the grace of finally looking into God's essence. And this Bernard does three times, by inviting Dante to lift up his eyes to the Queen immediately after the poet recognizes him (XXXI, 115–17), by talking about her at the beginning of Canto XXXII and again asking the pilgrim to gaze into the face which alone can prepare him to see Christ (XXXII, 85–7), and finally by praying to her on his behalf, as a spokesman followed by his "affection" (XXXII, 147–51; XXXIII, 1–39).

To these three invitations on Bernard's part correspond three successive stages of Dante's vision of the Virgin – what Chiappelli has called the "polyptych of the Mother".[3] We shall soon return to this image and its implications. But first we must pause to glance briefly at the poetic logic which, together with theo-

---

3. F. Chiappelli, "La struttura figurativa del 'Paradiso'", now in his *Il Legame Musaico* (Rome, 1984), pp. 126–8.

logical reasons, rules the gradual focussing of Dante's attention on Mary. In the last cantos of the *Comedy* Dante passes from Beatrice's guidance to that of Bernard and, finally, simply follows Mary's gaze into the "eternal light" (XXXIII, 43–8). Neither Beatrice nor Bernard are absent even from the last phases of this movement towards Mary and God. Indeed, Beatrice joins Bernard in his prayer to the Virgin (XXXIII, 38–9), and Bernard himself, after constantly urging Dante towards Mary and pronouncing his "santa orazione", signs to him with a smile to look upward into God (XXXIII, 49–51). But there is no doubt that while Beatrice is now distant from a Dante who has pronounced a valediction towards her and while Bernard is only an instrument, the last stage of Dante's journey before the 'visio Dei' is dominated by the Virgin. Though she remains present, Beatrice has been replaced, or is being supplemented by Mary, the true "donna" (XXXIII, 13) – Lady and Queen – of the highest Empyrean. The love incarnated by Beatrice, a love which, sprung on earth, partakes of Heaven as well, is now transcended by the Virgin's love (XXXIII, 7) before being sublimated and becoming one with "l'amor che move il sole e l'altre stelle".

This shift, theologically appropriate, has a deep *raison d'etre* in the architectural fabric of the poem. In the thrones around and under Mary there shine, together with Eve, John the Baptist, St Peter and others, Beatrice and Lucy, who, as Bernard reminds Dante, "moved [his] lady when [he] was bending [his] brows downward to [his] ruin" (XXXII, 137–8). What is recalled here is in fact the original impulse that sets the poem, and Dante's salvation, in motion. In *Inferno* II, when Dante seems on the point of giving up the journey that has been proposed to him as the only way of escaping from the dark wood, Virgil reveals why he has come to save him. In the course of this explanation (52–120) we learn that it was Mary herself who sent Lucy to Beatrice that she may help Dante (II, 94–108). Beatrice, in turn, asked Virgil to act as Dante's first guide (58–72; 115–20). Thus, the *Divine Comedy* presents a double movement – from Mary through Lucy and Beatrice to Virgil, and from Virgil to Beatrice, Bernard and Lucy, to Mary.

The Virgin is at the beginning and end, and, as has been shown by others, throughout the poem.[4] When, in *Purgatorio* V, Buonconte da Montefeltro arrives, after the battle of Campaldino, with a hole in his throat, spilling blood on the ground, where the Archiano flows into the Arno, he loses his

4. See M. Apollonio, s.v. "Maria Vergine", in *Enciclopedia Dantesca*, III, (Rome, 1971), pp. 835–9.

sight and speech, but dies "in the name of Mary", invoking her. And this "small tear" of repentance, this final silent prayer to Mary in the hour of his death ("ora pro nobis peccatoribus nunc et in hora mortis nostrae", says the *Ave Maria*) saves Buonconte's soul.

The triumph of Mary, however, begins in *Paradiso* XXIII, when, in the eighth circle of Heaven, Dante's mind, "made greater" than before, goes out of itself (43–5) in contemplating the light of Christ and the transfigured smile of Beatrice. There, in the "beautiful garden" "which blossoms beneath the rays of Jesus' is "la rosa in che 'l verbo divino carne si fece" (73–4), as Beatrice tells Dante. And at the mention of her name the poet fixes his sight upon her "fire". The "living star" is mirrored in his eyes, and Mary's apotheosis reaches its climax. A torch, the archangel Gabriel, descends through the heaven, forming a circle in the likeness of a crown that girds her and wheels about her. An ineffable melody surrounds "il bel zaffiro del quale il ciel più chiaro s'inzaffira". Gabriel celebrates in his holy dance "the supreme joy that breathes from out the womb which was the hostelry of our Desire", and circles around the Virgin until she follows her Son up to the highest sphere. All the other lights make Mary's name resound, while her "crowned flame" mounts upward after her "seed" – Christ. The blessed reach their lights upward, showing the love they bear to the Virgin, "like an infant which, when it has taken the milk, stretches its arms toward its mother" "per l'animo che 'nfin di fuor s'infiamma" – the first of the three similes with the image of mother and child at their centre that Dante uses in the final section of the *Paradiso*.[5] The *Regina coeli* resounds as Mary finally ascends to the Empyrean and St Peter appears (58–139).

"Figurando il paradiso", the "sacred poem" does indeed "make a leap" (61–3) here. Anticipating the beatific vision of Canto XXXIII,[6] it calls Mary "stella" as in the litanies,[7] proclaims her superior to any other creature,[8] alludes to the Incarnation three times (73–4, 104–5, 119–20), and in short sets her at the centre of our attention by means of a holy pageant where elements of earthly ceremonial and liturgy, and mystical vision, are fused.

This scene is reenacted and widened when Dante reaches the Empyrean, in the triptych I mentioned a while ago. In Canto XXXI, at the end of the recognition scene between Dante and Bernard, the play of light and fire which

5. The other two are *Paradiso* XXX, 82–4, and XXXIII, 107–8.
6. See *Paradiso*, XXIII, 49–51, and XXXIII, 58–63.
7. *Paradiso*, XXIII, 92. Mary is called "stella matutina" and "maris stella".
8. *Paradiso*, XXIII, 93; and cf. XXXIII, 1–6.

dominates the whole of the *Paradiso* is intensified by two similes that compare the splendour of Mary on the background of the general effulgence of the blessed to the fiery shining of the eastern sky at dawn:

> Io levai li occhi; e come da mattina
> la parte oriental de l'orizzonte
> soverchia quella dove 'l sol declina,
> cosí, quasi di valle andando a monte
> con li occhi, vidi parte ne lo stremo
> vincer di lume tutta l'altra fronte.
> E come quivi ove s'aspetta il temo
> che mal guidò Fetonte, piú s'infiamma,
> e quinci e quindi il lume si fa scemo,
> cosí quella pacifica oriafiamma
> nel mezzo s'avvivava, e d'ogne parte
> per igual modo allentava la fiamma ...

> (I lifted up my eyes; and as at morning
> the eastern parts of the horizon outshine
> that where the sun declines, so, as if
> going with my eyes from valley to
> mountain-top I saw a part on the ex-
> treme verge surpass with its light all the
> rest of the rim. And as the point where
> we await the pole that Phaethon mis-
> guided is most aglow, and on this side
> and on that the light diminishes, so was
> that pacific oriflamme quickened in the
> middle, on either side in equal measure
> tempering its flame; 118–29).

Mary is indeed "stella matutina", but the magnificent articulation of the dawn image recalls other key moments of the poem – the beginning itself of the journey (*Inferno*, I, 37–40), which is echoed, too, in that movement of the eyes from valley to mountain-top (*Inferno*, I, 13–18); the arrival on the shores of Purgatory, when the "bel pianeto che d'amar conforta faceva tutto rider l'oriente" (I, 19–20); and the appearance of Beatrice in the Earthly Paradise (*Purgatorio*, XXX, 22–4).

Here, more than a thousand feasting angels converge towards Mary with open wings and Dante sees the Virgin smile ineffably at their games and songs. The actual expression he uses – "ridere una bellezza" (134) – is a contrapuntal reminiscence of *Purgatorio* I. It once more condenses human and divine and makes Mary's face radiate forth in and be mirrored by the eyes of all the saints. In the "caldo suo calor" Dante's own gaze is now fixed, as if in anticipation of Bernard's praise of that warmth in *Paradiso* XXXIII (7–9).

When Canto XXXII begins, Bernard, the "contemplante", becomes a "doctor" — a "magister" — and illustrates to his pupil the structure of the mystical rose, at the centre of which sits Mary, whose historical function of healer of the wound inflicted by Eve (who now shines at the Virgin's feet) is recalled at the opening of the Canto (4–6). This historical function is sublimated and transposed onto eternity by the reenacting of the Annunciation that constitutes the second scene of the triptych. Here, Gabriel descends before Mary and, spreading his wings, sings "Ave Maria, gratia plena". The whole blessed Court responds to the "divina cantilena" (94–9). To contemplate the Virgin in this context means to become ready to see Christ, for hers is the face that most resembles His, and Bernard once more underlines the central importance of the Incarnation when he explains to Dante that it is Gabriel who "looks into the eyes of our Queen", "so enamoured that he seems afire" (103–4), precisely because he it was "who bore the palm down to Mary, when the Son of God willed to load Himself with the burden of our flesh" (112–14).

It is, then, in this context that Dante inserts the prayer to the Virgin of *Paradiso* XXXIII — as part of the innermost texture of the entire poem, as the last stage of the transformation of the protagonist's love, as a preparation for his supreme experience, the vision of God. Mary's triumphs are the last appearances of a human being, however now transfigured, in the poem, because Mary represents the point where human and divine have met in the flesh, changing the world's history. This is why she acquires more and more prominence, and why Bernard now addresses her.

This tie between history and eternity is the theme of Bernard's prayer.[9] Its first part (1–21), which constitutes a traditionally formal *elogium*, or praise of the Virgin, is a) an illustration of the history of man's salvation (1–9), and b) a praise of Mary as intermediary between man and God, of her role for men on earth and for the blessed in Heaven (10–21). The second section of Bernard's speech (22–39) is his prayer on behalf of Dante and it recounts the story of Dante's own salvation from time to eternity. In the first nine lines of the prayer, history is seen and interpreted by a divine measure, as an element of an eternal plan. From line 10 to line 21 God's grace is shown as acting, through Mary's person, both in time, on earth, and beyond time, in Heaven. Finally, in the last section of the prayer, the history of man's salvation becomes the story of one man's salvation: the grace of God has, through Mary, acted upon Dante and brought him to Heaven. This grace is now invoked, through Mary ("per grazia", 25), so that Dante may be enabled to attain ultimate salvation, the contemplation of God with his own, human eyes.

9. I reproduce here, with corrections, a shortened version of the first part of my "The Sibyl's Leaves: A Study of *Paradiso* XXXIII", *Dante Studies*, XCVI (1978), 83–126.

What is presented to us in the first six verses is the historical side of God's incarnation: the meta-historical, eternal mystery of this Incarnation will be contemplated later in the canto (127–32). Mary is the human medium of man's salvation as foreordained by God: "ab aeterno ordinata sum", as the Bible says.[10] Dante makes this explicit in the central line of the opening:

> termine fisso d'etterno consiglio.

Mary is the terminal point of eternal counsel, the goal in time of a plan conceived out of time. We have, then, in these two *terzine*, a straight line from Creation to Incarnation, from "fattore", the Maker, through human nature ("umana natura", 4), to "fattura", Its making, a creature of flesh and blood, the Son of Man. Human nature was ennobled and ransomed through Mary, a virgin humble and therefore, according to the Gospels, exalted above all creatures ("umile e alta").[11] Upon Mary came the Holy Ghost, one of whose names, according to the theologians,[12] is *Amor*, Love. Hence, in Mary's womb was rekindled love:[13]

> nel ventre tuo si raccese l'amore.

Mary's womb was the key to God's love: Mary herself was, as Dante says in the *Purgatorio* (X, 41–42),

> . . . quella
> ch'ad aprir l'alto amor volse la chiave.

Mary reopened God's love for man. But only through her own love and humility did God take flesh. Mary's acceptance of the Divine burden was man's supreme act of love. Thus Mary's womb was the meeting point of human and divine love.

Once the Incarnation took place, the way to God was open. In the third *terzina* of the canto we then have a straight line from Incarnation to beatitude in God, from history to eternity. God's love, rekindled in Mary's womb, makes it possible for men to raise themselves to Him and rest in the eternal peace of the mystical rose. The straight line, here, implies Christ's passion, crucifixion, and resurrection, through which man was saved and shown the way past death to eternal life:

---

10. Proverbs 8. 22–30.
11. Matthew 23.12, and, in particular for Mary, Luke 1.46–49.
12. See, for instance, Thomas Aquinas, *Summa Theologiae*, I, q. 37, a. 1.
13. And see *Convivio*, IV, v, 3.

Nel ventre tuo si raccese l'amore
per lo cui caldo nell'etterna pace
così è germinato questo fiore.

From line 1 to line 9 the circle is then complete: from God to God, from the eternity of Creation through history to the eternity of beatitude.

Until now Bernard has, in his *elogium*, praised Mary as the historical mediator between man and God: now, in lines 10–15, is celebrated Mary's eternal function. Torch of charity for those saved, for the blessed (10–11), and spring of hope for those who are to be saved, for mortal men (11–12), Mary is the medium of God's grace:

che qual vuol grazia ed a te non ricorre,
sua disianza vuol volar sanz'ali.

The past tense used in the first eight lines of the canto is abandoned as soon as Bernard comes to the mystical flower of the Empyrean: the present is used afterwards, to indicate the ever present role of Mary. The passage is smooth and takes place by association of ideas: the first movement ends with "questo fiore", indicating the Empyrean; the second begins with "qui", indicating the Empyrean again.

Bernard's praise now mounts in crescendo, pausing on Mary's own qualities: loving-kindness, mercy, pity, bounty. Mary is, then, the epitome of all creatures' goodness:

. . . in te s'aduna
quantunque in creatura è di bontate.

At the same time, Bernard lays the ground for the request that forms the second part of the prayer. He reminds Mary that only through her can Dante obtain the final vision. Her qualities should prepare her to grant Dante his final request. In celebrating Mary's "benignità", Bernard says that many times it freely anticipates the asking. This is not only true in general. It is particularly true for Dante, who, as we have seen, was saved by her intervention when he was lost in the dark wood of sin. She is the Grace at the beginning and end of Dante's journey.

This journey is now recalled by Bernard: from the "infima lacuna dell'universo" to the Empyrean, Dante has seen the lives of the spirits one by one. He has come all the way from the river over which the sea has no boast of *Inferno* II to the river out of which issue living sparks, the Empyrean. It was the journey that Virgil had proposed to him, and Dante is now at the end of it. There is, in Bernard's words here (22–4), a heaviness, underlined by the enjambment and by the slow "ad una ad una" which does not express tiredness, but all the weight of the experience conquered by Dante. It is of all the journey, of all this experience that Mary — and we with her — are reminded. The entire poem is summed up before its end.

This recalling is, however, functional: it constitutes the poem to Bernard's requests on behalf of Dante. Here, then, the praise becomes prayer, the *elogium, supplicatio*. Bernard's requests are basically two: the first, expressed in lines 22–23, regards Dante's immediate objective, the attainment of ultimate salvation with the vision of God; the second, expressed in lines 34–36, regards Dante's future, the stability of his "affetti" after the beatific vision. Bernard's first request is, however, articulated in two moments, which are separated both formally and substantially. In the first, Bernard presents his request as a mere interpreter of Dante's own wishes: "Or *questi* ... supplica a te". In the second, it is Bernard himself who prays to the Virgin, underlining his request with rhetorical emphasis: "E *io* ... tutti miei prieghi ti porgo, e priego che non sieno scarsi". What Dante asks through Bernard is to receive, by divine grace, so much power that he can raise himself with his eyes to the "ultima salute". Through Bernard, Dante asks for the supreme Object. Bernard, in his own request, emphasizes the subjective means for the attainment of this Object. He asks Mary to disperse every cloud of Dante's mortality, so that the supreme joy may be disclosed to him. In other words, Bernard asks Mary to grant Dante the last *trasumanar*, the final stage of that passing beyond humanity which had begun in the first canto of *Paradiso*. Here we have the announcement of the central themes of Canto XXXIII: the sight of the Object and the progressive passing beyond humanity of the seer, the subject. At the same time, both the subjective and objective aspects of the final goal are indicated by the two expressions, "ultima salute" and "sommo piacer". God is, in Himself, both *salvatio* and *diligibile*;[14] yet ultimate salvation and supreme pleasure are Dante's own, subjective ends. "Piacer", in particular, indicates the main dimension of Dante's feelings in Canto XXXIII of *Paradiso*.[15]

Bernard's third request refers to Dante's future: this, too, is presented as the saint's own preoccupation ("Ancor ti prego"). What the last guide asks is that, after the overwhelming vision, Dante's "affetti" may remain "sani". It is clear that Bernard refers to Dante's inclinations, which must be kept pure even

---

14. See S. Thomas Aquinatis *In Librum Beati Dionysii De Divinis Nominibus Expositio*, I, Lectio iii, 98.
15. See "dolce" and "godo" later in the Canto (63, 93).

after the vision in order for Dante to avoid sinning again. The vision in itself is no guarantee against a new fall. But "affetti" has a wider meaning: it implies passion, feeling, state of mind, will. And "sani" means not only 'pure', but also 'wholesome'. Bernard, then, asks Mary to grant Dante his integrity as man and poet after the beatific vision.

Finally, Bernard passes from indirect prayer to direct exhortation:

> Vinca tua guardia i movimenti umani.

This line introduces the last stage of the prayer, which is now choral. It is not just Bernard and Dante, but also Beatrice and all the blessed who pray to Mary. "Vedi", says Bernard to Mary, and indirectly we see the silent congregation clasp their hands. Not a word is spoken, but a gesture is glanced at — the hieratic gesture of medieval painting. The rest of the canto is silent, and we only follow sight: Mary's eyes fixed on Bernard (40—41), then on God (43—45) — only their movement meaning acceptance of the prayer and address to God for intercession. Bernard's eyes sign to Dante to look upward (49—50), but Dante's eyes are already fixed on God (50—4). And here, with Dante's vista we pass into the second section of the canto.

The first — and lasting — impression that this prayer makes on the reader and even more on the listener is that of a severity and solemnity behind which burns an extraordinary ardour. The antitheses of the first two verses — virgin, mother, daughter of thy Son, etc. — are based upon totally abstract, dogmatic definitions. It is on the intellectual level that we receive Bernard's message. In the third verse, "termine fisso d'etterno consiglio", the antithesis is more subtle, for it rests on a less directly identifiable contrast of 'fixed goal' and 'eternal'. But the effect is, again, purely intellectual. There is no doubt that this is 'austere' poetry. Part of its appeal rests precisely on this. But there is more. In the first place, we realize that these three verses constitute just an invocation. What Bernard accumulates here are four vocatives, which provide his opening words with great solemnity and majesty. To this we must add the effect of the rhetorical antitheses themselves, which produce vivacity within the severity. Finally, we must consider the internal, grammatical balancing out of these antitheses: the first is based on a contraposition of two nouns ("vergine" — "madre"), the third of two adjectives ("umile" — "alta"); the second results from a contrast between a noun in the vocative and a noun in the genitive ("figlia del tuo figlio"), accompanied by a possessive adjective ("tuo") which grammatically refers to the genitive ("figlio") but conceptually to the vocative ("figlia"); the fourth has the same structure of the second, with a noun in the vocative ("termine") and a noun in the genitive ("consiglio"), but the contraposition is based on the adjectives that accompany both ("fisso" – "eterno"). The distribution is perfect:

> Vergine Madre, figlia del tuo figlio
> umile e alta più che creatura,
> termine fisso d'etterno consiglio ...

But this is not all. The third line ("termine fisso d'etterno consiglio") sums up the meaning of the first two: Mary is the fixed goal of eternal counsel inasmuch as she is virgin and mother, daughter of her Son, humble and exalted. At the same time, she is virgin and mother, daughter of her Son, humble and exalted precisely because she is 'ordinata ab aeterno' to be the goal of a divine plan. When we add to all this the echoes of the Gospels, of the Old Testament, of Bernard's own sermons that Dante has adapted and condensed in these three lines,[16] we begin to understand the nature of this poetry. These verses have no halo of vagueness around them: the terms are very precise and imply well-defined concepts. But the reverberation they have on each other and their concentration in three verses produce an effect of extraordinary intensity. When the period, in the following tercet, is brought to completion, Bernard's thought widens itself in a slow circumlocution: two enjambments make it pause and revolve upon itself. The antithesis ("fattore" – "fattura") is resolved through the verb ("non disdegnò di farsi"). The verb itself placates the tension: Dante does not simply say: 'the Maker made Himself its [human natura's] making'. Dante says: "the Maker did not disdain to make Himself its making". Yet, though more articulate than the preceding one, the phrase is no less compact. Its second section ("che 'l suo fattore ...") is a consecutive clause dependent on the first part ("nobilitasti sí"), and the two possessive adjectives ("suo" and "sua"), which refer to the subject and the object of the consecutive clause, are tied up to the object ("umana natura") of the principal. In the principal the subject, the anaphorical "tu", opens the sentence, thus emphasizing the person of the addressee; but then the object ("umana natura") precedes the verb, so that the stress falls on it. In the consecutive clause, the tension produced by this inversion disappears; here, the sequence is the normal one: subject ("fattore"), verb ("non disdegnò di farsi"), predicate-object ("fattura"):

> tu se' colei che l'umana natura
> nobilitasti sí, che 'l suo fattore
> non disdegnò di farsi sua fattura.

16. For these, see the comments on the canto by modern editors, in particular those by Scartazzini-Vandelli, Casini-Barbi, and Sapegno.

The explosion of images and metaphors in the next tercet reveals, however, that the tension is stronger than ever:

> Nel ventre tuo si raccese l'amore,
> per lo cui caldo ne l'etterna pace
> cosí è germinato questo fiore.

The field is defined by the images of generation ("ventre" and "germinato") and fire ("raccese" and "caldo"). The interaction of these images makes us feel as if in Mary's womb an explosion had taken place, the heat of which arouses life and pervades the universe. It is as if we were witnessing the action of the sun through the millennia — its rekindling after ages of darkness and cold, its heat radiating through space and time and finally causing the flower to grow. The movement is indeed, as we have seen, through time: from Incarnation to beatitude. But the image suggests more. We do not merely have generation and fire: we also have 'eternal peace' and 'flower'. There is some kind of reverberation of the first verse into the third, as if an analogy were implied — and "cosí" might have a shade of the 'cosí' of similes. The analogy implied by this reverberation is between the rekindling of love in Mary's womb and the germinating, the blooming of the flower in the eternal peace: in this manner, the rekindling of love in a woman's womb acquires a shadow of vegetable life, and viceversa, the blooming of the flower becomes like an explosion of fire. Here again, Dante has adapted expressions derived from Church writers,[17] has perfected images which he had already used,[18] but he has inserted them in a wider, more compact context.

From this moment on, the image of fire and burning pervades this section of the canto: Mary is a noonday *torch* (10–11), Bernard *burns* for Dante's vision (28–9), Dante himself ends the *ardour* of his craving (48). When Bernard says, "E io, che mai per mio veder non arsi", he makes explicit precisely that ardour which, as I have said, shows itself in the images that enlighten the austerity of his words: the torch of charity, the spring of hope, the flying without wings, the "infima lacuna dell'universo", the cloud of mortality. One cannot fail to notice a particular flickering of the flame of emotion, for instance, when Dante mentions that "infima lacuna dell'universo" by which, with remote detachment, he expresses all together the sensations of bottom, emptiness,

---

17. For lines 7–9 see St Ambrose, *De iust. Virg.*, 91, and St Bernard, *Serm. in adv. Dom.*, II, 4.
18. See *Paradiso*, XXII, 47–8.

lagoon and lake of Cocytus.[19] The ardour shows in the accumulation of abstract nouns which define the virtues of Mary, with the iteration of "in te"; in the repetition of "prego" in lines 29–32; in the final, direct exhortation to the Virgin. It is the mixture of historical, dogmatic, figural, emotional and rhetorical elements[20] that determines the intensity of this ardour. It is this eloquence that became a model, which, as we shall soon see, appealed to Petrarch and Chaucer. It is this ardour that paves the way to the seeing silence which reigns in Canto XXXIII of *Paradiso*.

Mary's eyes, those eyes "beloved and reverenced by God", are fixed on the "orator", thus "showing how greatly devout prayers please her" (40–2). Then, with a sudden, silent shift, they turn to the Eternal Light (43–5). And this simple gesture makes Dante approach the paroxism of his desire:

> E io ch'al fine di tutt' i disii
> appropinquava, sí com'io dovea,
> l'ardor del desiderio in me finii.
> (46–8)

The language of earthly love becomes the language of the beatific vision. Henceforth, Dante's sight penetrates and sinks through the essence of God, sharpening his memory and poetic medium until his will and his desire, which we have seen raised to the utmost after the prayer to the Virgin, are revolved by

> l'amor che move il sole e l'altre stelle.[21]

Though in a completely different manner, the prayer to the Virgin, if not Mary herself, occupies an important place in the story of another fourteenth-century pilgrimage, the *Pèlerinage de la Vie Humaine* of Guillaume de Deguileville, of which the author himself compiled two different versions, one dating back to 1331, and another to 1355. In both redactions, the story, narrated in purely allegorical terms, is represented by the earthly adventures of a man who, having seen the Heavenly Jerusalem in a vision, decides to undertake a pilgrimage thither. Helped by Grace Dieu in his many troubles, the pilgrim goes through life until Age and Sickness, the precursors of Death, warn him of his approach and, while Prayer comes as a guide, he finally wakes up.

19. "Infima" indicates the bottom; "lacuna" = 'emptiness'; "lacuna" = 'laguna' (lagoon) and hence the lake of Cocytus at the bottom of Hell and of the universe.
20. For a thorough analysis of these, see E. Auerbach, "Dante's Prayer", and M. Fubini, *Due studi danteschi* (Florence, 1951), pp. 63–82.
21. I have examined this vision in "The Sibyl's Leaves", for which see note 9 above.

It is impossible to do justice to, or examine in detail, this monumental work here.[22] Suffice it to say that while in our own century it has been taken as a paradigm of medieval allegorical fiction,[23] it seems to have been extremely popular throughout Europe from the fourteenth through the fifteenth down to the beginning of the seventeenth century. Starting in 1426, Lydgate translated and adapted the second, and longer, version into English, and it is his rendering that I shall use here.[24]

In this version we have three prayers to the Virgin. The first occurs rather early in the poem (after line 7188 in a total of 24832), after the pilgrim's meeting with Lady Reason and Moses. Nature has a long argument with Grace Dieu over transubstantiation in the Eucharist, which she obviously cannot tolerate (how can bread and wine not remain bread and wine?), and resorts to her clerk Aristotle, who debates with, and is defeated by, Sapientia. At this point Grace Dieu hands the pilgrim a scroll which contains a Latin poem on the Trinity (*Pater, creator omnium*) and a longer hymn, in Latin, to the Virgin Mary (*Ave reclinatorium*). Here, the *elogium* celebrates the Mother of God as she who changed Eve's "damnatorium" into joy (1–12), as the reference point for all men who are lost (13–24), the most splendid of stars, humble in prosperity and strong in adversity (25–36). Gradually, the images focus on Mary as the receptacle of the divine seed. Announced in stanza 8 ("Tu divine imaginis, Et eterni es luminis Beatum receptaculum", 88–90), this theme reaches its climax towards the end of the hymn, where the birth and death of Christ are linked to the Eucharist, and this in turn, through the image of the fruit, to Mary's womb and to her virginity, the "flower" which she kept together with the "fructus":

> Benedictus in seculum   Sit ille per quem titulum
> Talem habes in seculo,   Christus, qui tui clausulum
> Vteri sui baiulum   Fecit firmato pessulo.
> Qui, moriens pro populo   Se dedit in patibulo
> Opprobij spectaculum;   Et, superato Zabulo,
> Fracto-que suo baculo,   Se suis dat in pabulum.

22. Editions of the *Pélerinage:* first version, ed. J.J. Sturzinger (Roxburghe Club, 1893); second version, eds. B. and J. Petit (Paris, ca. 1500); ed. A. Verard (Paris, 1511). An English prose translation of the first version was edited by W.A. Wright for the Roxburghe Club in 1869.
23. R. Tuve, *Allegorical Imagery* (Princeton, 1966), pp. 145–218. Tuve writes about the first, more compact and artistically more balanced version, where I have been able to find only one prayer to the Virgin, the original of Chaucer's *ABC*.
24. The edition of Lydgate's *Pilgrimage* is by F.J. Furnivall and K.B. Locock, EETS, ES 77, 83, 92 (London, 1899–1904).

Fructus est comestibilis,   Comedentibus vtilis,
Dulcis anime gustui,   Nature ammirabilis,
Arti indoctrinabilis,   Stupendus intellectui,
Inusitatus vsui,   Vetito quondam fructui;
In omnibus dissimilis   Solummodo auditui,
Et non alteri sensui   Fide comprensibilis.

Ventris tui in ortulo,   Ornato flore primulo,
Iste fructus colligitur;   Sed, ut vultus in speculo
Representatur oculo,   Et speculum non leditur,
Sic dum a te recipitur,   Dum manet; dum egreditur,
Hoc sit illeso claustrulo: Nulla via relinquitur,
Nil suspectum admittitur;   Fructum habes cum flosculo.

(121–56; stanzas 11–13)

There is no doubt that this is Grace Dieu's answer to Nature and Aristotle: the mysteries here concentrated in a few lines are indeed "wonderful to nature, unteachable to art", and comprehensible only to faith (136–7, 144). And this is precisely the reason why this hymn is inserted here together with the *Pater, creator omnium*, where the Trinity is extolled.

The second prayer to the Virgin is part of a different context. When, after choosing the right path on the advice of Moral Virtue, the pilgrim is led astray by Youth, he meets Gluttony, Venus and Sloth, then Pride and Envy, and finally Wrath and Tribulation. Attacked by all these in turn, the protagonist defends himself by appealing to Mary (16275–16978).

As in Dante's case, though in a more pedantic manner, St Bernard is the intermediary. The *Pilgrimage* inserts here an English version of Bernard's homily "De Laudibus Virginis Matris Super Verba Evangelii *Missus est angelus Gabriel*", making it end with a ballad on the Virgin.[25] Once more, the purpose of both is clear in the context of the narrative. Recourse to Mary saves man from sin and protects him in tribulation. With the magnificent rhetoric that characterizes his fervent prose, St Bernard expounds in his homily the Gospel of the Annunciation, beginning with Adam and Eve, explaining the Old Testament prophecies and figures of Mary, the paradoxes of the Incarnation, and the name of the Virgin. 'Maria' is 'Maris stella' for indeed her rays shine on the

---

25. Sancti Bernardí *Opera Omnia*, ed. J. Mabillon (Paris, 1690), III, 732–55. The prayer to the Virgin, which in Verard's edition is given in Latin, replaces a short prayer to God in the first redaction of the *Pélerinage*. In Petit's French edition the prose is absent and we have instead 113 French lines ("Et que me vint a remembrance", printed also by K.B. Locock in Part III of the EETS edition of Lydgate, ES 92, pp. 684–5), which use various passages from St. Bernard.

entire universe, her splendour pervades Heaven, penetrates Hell, and runs through the Earth inflaming human minds. The 'cohortatio ad cultum' follows this last eulogy. I quote a section of it from the original Latin to give an idea of the style which inspired Dante and countless other medieval authors:

> O quisquis te intelligis in hujus saeculi profluvio magis inter procellas et tempestates fluctuare, quam per terram ambulare; ne avertas oculos a fulgore hujus sideris, si non vis obrui procellas. Si insurgant venti *tentationum*, si incurras scopulos *tribulationum:* respice stellam, voca Mariam. Si jactaris superbiae *undis*, si ambitionis, si detractionis, si aemulationis; respice stellam, voca Mariam. Si iracundia, aut avaritia, aut carnis illecebra *naviculam* concusserit mentis; respice ad Mariam …[26]

We shall soon see how the image of the sea prompts the pilgrim to pray to Mary once more. Here, it is evident that Bernard's exhortations fit the plight of the pilgrim attacked by various temptations (pride, envy, wrath, avarice and lust in the Homily's order) and above all faced by the 'rocks of tribulation'. It is Mary as 'Refuge in Tribulation' that the Ballad at the end of the prose tract invokes, making each of the four stanzas end with the word "trybulacion". Here is the third, where several of St Bernard's images recur:

> O holy Sterre / ffyx in stabylnesse,
> With-oute Eclypsyng / Or Mutabylyte,
> Ylyche Clere / shynyng in bryghtnesse,
> In whom the Sonne / sent ffro the deyete,
> lyste ffor to take / Oure humanyte,
> Off Mankynde / to make Redempcion,
> That thow shuldest / O mayde, O Moder ffre,
> Be Oure Reffuge / In trybulacion!
>
> (16963–70, stanza 3)

The next prayer to the Virgin comes shortly afterwards (19791), as the pilgrim, having met Avarice and Heresy and talked to Satan, tries to swim across the sea because the devil blocks all other routes. This time, Mary's help is invoked with even greater urgency in a poem which, 276 lines long in the French original, has been reduced to 184 in the English translation. The surprise is that the English version is not by Lydgate, but by Chaucer, whom the monk of Bury acknowledges and celebrates before reverently quoting his *ABC*.

Here, we have an instance of the transformations that literary forms undergo in the Middle Ages. The *ABC*, itself but an example of the many 'Abecedaria'

---

26. St Bernard, *Opera*, III, 743. Italics mine.

in honour of Mary such as those collected in the *Analecta Hymnica Medii Aevi*, is used by Deguileville as a lyrical utterance serving the purposes of a narrative. As in the two previous instances of prayers to the Virgin, the pilgrim invokes Mary as the only source of help in his distress:

> A toy du monde le refui,
> Vierge glorieuse, m'en fui
> Tout confus, ne puis miex faire;
> A toy me tien, a toy m'apuy.
> Relieve moy, abatu suy:
> Vaincu m'a mon aversaire.
>
> $(1-6)^{27}$

Elaborate as it is, the *elogium* that follows these lines is always also *supplicatio* — indeed in each stanza the last lines seem to focus on the protagonist's condition. Now, if the tradition recorded in Speght's edition of Chaucer is correct, the *ABC* was translated and adapted by the English poet "at the request of Blanche, Duchess of Lancaster, as a prayer for her private use".[28] In any case, Chaucer's *ABC* is a purely lyrical piece, and the transformations it has undergone in passing from French to English respond to this new purpose. Both Wolfgang Clemen and Patricia Kean remarked that Chaucer's version shows "a greater intensity conveyed by heightened expression" and a strengthening and simplification of the thematic material.[29] At the same time, the 'I' behind the urgency of the French *Pélerinage* (and of Lydgate's *Pilgrimage*) has become impersonal. The *ABC* is a prayer that can be used by anyone — it is as if Dante's St Bernard had stopped at line 21 of his *elogium* and then attached on to it a general request of help and mercy.

Moreover, if we look at the *ABC* in the light of Auerbach's distinction between dogmatic, historical, figural and emotional elements and their developments in medieval eulogies of the Virgin,[30] we immediately realize that not only "there is no consecutive thread running through the poem",[31] but the dogmatic element is diluted throughout the composition, and only six stanzas out of twenty-three present either historical or figural ideas. Thus the sorrow

27. The French original of the *ABC* is printed also by W.W. Skeat in his *Complete Works of Geoffrey Chaucer* (London, repr. 1963), I, pp. 261–71.
28. F.N. Robinson in his second edn. of Chaucer's *Works* (London, 1966), p. 520.
29. W.H. Clemen, *Chaucer's Early Poetry* (London, 1963), pp. 175–9 (quotation, p. 175); P.M. Kean, *Chaucer and the Making of English Poetry*, II (London, 1972), pp. 193–6. See also A. David, "An ABC To the Style of the Prioress", in M.J. Carruthers and E.D. Kirk, eds., *Acts of Interpretation: The Text in Its Contexts, 700–1600* (Norman, Oklahoma, 1982), pp. 147–57.
30. For which see Auerbach, "Dante's Prayer".
31. Kean, *Chaucer*, p. 193.

of Mary under the cross is recalled at lines 81–2, but only to be appealed to, that the foe might not prevail against it and render vain what Christ and His mother "have bought so deere". The burning bush of Moses, "signe" and "figure" of Mary's "unwemmed maidenhede" receiving the Holy Ghost (89–94) is evoked simply in order to be associated with the fire "that in helle eternalli shal dure", from which Mary should defend us (95–6). The meditation on "wherfore and whi the Holi Gost thee soughte, Whan Gabrielles vois cam to thin ere" (114–15) is abandoned after a few lines. Christ's Passion and the figure of Longinus (unnamed in Deguileville) are mentioned only to be contrasted to the sinner's falseness and unkindness (161–8). Isaac was the "figure" of Jesus' sacrifice (169–72), but this is only the "measure" of the mercy that is invoked (173–6). Zechariah's words (13.1), "In that day there shall be a fountain opened to the house of David and to the inhabitants of Jerusalem for sin and uncleanness", generally applied to the blood of Christ as in Revelation 1.5, are here figurally related to the Virgin (177–8), but the rest of the last stanza draws from this the rather abrupt conclusion that "nere thi tender herte, we were spilt" (180).[32] Chaucer does indeed, as Wolpers and Clemen have observed,[33] go beyond doctrinal limits, "ascribing to the Virgin the epithet 'Almighty' which is rightly applicable to none but God alone", and this "in his very first address"; but the rest of his epithets concentrate on the idea of Mary as 'Queen' (24, 25, 77, 97, 121, 149) – "glorious mayde and mooder" and "temple devout" (49, 145) being the only two exceptions.

There are, however, at least two sections of the *ABC* where Chaucer goes far beyond the original of Deguileville. In stanzas 13 and 14 of his version, the 'N' and 'O' of the alphabet, Chaucer seems to explore the possibilities inherent in two different ways of dealing with the traditional Marian eulogy. In the first, after calling Mary "advocat" according to the *Salve Regina*, he points to the fact that the Virgin helps men but "for litel hire":

> We han noon oother melodye or glee
> Us to rejoyse in oure adversitee,
> Ne advocat noon that wole and dar so preye
> For us, and that for litel hire as yee,
> That helpen for an Ave-Marie or tweye.
> (100–104)

32. The French is simpler, but more effective:
    Fontaine patent te nomme
    Pour laver pecheur homme:
    . . .
    Moy laver veillez entendre,
    Moy garder et moy deffendre . . . (268–75; Skeat).
33. Clemen, pp. 176–7 (the following quotation is from this). And see T. Wolpers, "Geschichte der englischen Marienlyrik im Mittelalter", *Anglia*, LXIX (1950), p. 29.

The last line of this passage (which is totally different in the French original) slightly jars with the solemn intonation of the rest of the poem and particularly with the rhetorical sweep of the next stanza. In fact, it is a brief experiment in poetic simplicity and candour, in the 'humble' style that will characterize some of the *Canterbury Tales*, namely the Prioress's portrait of the little child who, whenever he saw "th'ymage Of Cristes mooder", used to kneel and "seye His *Ave Marie*, as he goth by the weye" (VII, 507–8). The intonation suddenly reminds us of Buonconte da Montefeltro's end "in the name of Mary" – the "lacrimetta" that snatches his soul from the devil's hands.

The next lines, instead, make use of a very different register. Here, the experiment is in the 'high' style of some traditional eulogies, where Auerbach's 'emotional' element is mixed with scriptural echoes ("ancilla Domini") and contrasts are established ("ancille" – "maistresse") to produce an invocation with the breath and vigour of those we shall hear in *Troilus*:

> O verrey light of eyen that ben blynde,
> O verrey lust of labour and distresse,
> O tresoreere of bountee to mankynde,
> Thee whom God ches to mooder for humblesse!
> From his ancille he made the maistresse
> Of hevene and erthe, oure bille up for to beede.
> (105–10)[34]

We will soon see where this kind of inspiration leads Chaucer once he comes into contact with Dante and can use the *elogium* to Mary in a narrative context. The *ABC*, a lyrical piece drawn from a French allegorical narrative and employed again in an English version, provides us with a good touchstone against which to measure Dante's use of Mary and of the Prayer to the Virgin in the story of his ascent to God. In both the *Divine Comedy* and the *Pélerinage*, recourse to Mary takes place at crucial moments, when the protagonist is in need of help. There are, however, three basic differences between Dante and Deguileville-Lydgate. In the first place, Deguileville's presentation has the appearance of flat 'literariness': the prayers to Mary come on a scroll, or as a quotation of Bernard's sermon, or as an 'abecedarium'. The medium is a purely 'literal' use of literature on an allegorical background. What counts is the message. In Dante, as we have seen, all this becomes 'dramatic': Bernard is a character, Mary triumphs in Heaven in a continuous play of lights, the Annunciation is reenacted, the images recall other key moments of the poem.

---

34. The French (Skeat, 157–68) is clearly the source here, but Chaucer has expanded, straightened out, and heightened it.

The medium complements and enriches the message. Secondly, there are differences in the message itself. In the *Pélerinage*, the first hymn to Mary is Grace Dieu's answer to the rationalistic speculations of Nature and Aristotle, but the other two prayers come from the soul of the prilgrim himself. In the *Divine Comedy*, Mary acts of her own accord when she sets in motion Lucy, Beatrice, and Virgil to save Dante:

> Donna è gentil nel ciel che si compiange
> di questo impedimento ov'io ti mando,
> sí che duro giudicio là su frange

> (In Heaven there is a gracious lady who has such
> pity of this impediment to which I send you that
> stern judgement is broken thereabove),

says Beatrice to Virgil (*Inferno*, II, 94–6). Mary's pity of Dante's "impediment" acts to 'break' the "stern judgement" of God, according to which Dante would be condemned. And indeed Bernard confirms in his prayer to the Virgin in *Paradiso* XXXIII that her "loving-kindness not only succours him who asks, but oftentimes freely foreruns the asking" (16–18). This Dantean Mary is in a way, as several early commentators pointed out,[35] the theological 'prevenient Grace'. Deguileville's pilgrim, and Chaucer's 'I' in the *ABC*, must *ask* for grace.[36] *Grace Dieu* does indeed appear at the beginning of the French poem, but she only points to the protagonist the truth of transubstantiation by handing him a scroll with a hymn to Mary. Finally, when at the end of his journey Dante, through Bernard, implores Mary "per grazia" (*Paradiso*, XXXIII, 25), he does so in order to be granted enough 'virtue' as to be capable of gazing into God's own essence – a request which is far from the mind of Deguileville's and Lydgate's pilgrim as well as from the lips of Chaucer's praying 'I'. The dreamer of the *Pélerinage* wakes up just before Death catches him. He prays to God, but never enters the Heavenly Jerusalem he saw at the beginning of his vision. What is possible in the world of Dante's poetry and theology is avoided, if not altogether impossible, in Deguileville's and Chaucer's. Nor, though he does contemplate the City of God, is the dreamer of *Pearl* allowed inside it. And the pilgrimage of Piers Plowman never ends.

35. For references, see Scartazzini-Vandelli, p. 17, n. 94. On 'prevenient grace' see, for instance, Thomas Aquinas, *Summa Theol.*, 1–2, q. 111, 3.
36. The idea of prevenient grace may be hinted at in *ABC* 66–8, and in the French original (Skeat, 97–102).

The *ABC* is, as I hope to have shown, a lyric that represents the form in a state of transition.[37] Starting with a French 'abecedarium', Chaucer explores several ways of dealing with his subject — 'historical', 'figural', 'emotional', 'humble' and 'high' — but settles on none. In this sense, it is completely different from Dante's prayer to the Virgin, in which all traditional forms are fused in a very tight whole by the control of a mature poet. The question we must ask ourselves now is, what does the greatest lyric poet of the fourteenth century do when he, too, writes his prayer to the Virgin?

In the *Canzoniere* such as we have it and such as he finally arranged it, Francis Petrarch, the "lauriat poete" of the *Clerk's Tale*, placed *Vergine bella* at the very end, as the last of the 366 lyrics that make up the collection. This choice, together with that of *Voi ch'ascoltate* to introduce the 'rime sparse', reveals that Petrarch thought carefully about the 'frame' of the *Canzoniere*, and that this frame has a decidedly 'penitential' character. In the first sonnet the poet recalls the sighs he used to utter "in his youthful error", asks for pity and forgiveness, and concludes with a confession:

> et del mio vaneggiar vergogna è 'l frutto,
> e 'l pentersi, e 'l conoscer chiaramente
> che quanto piace al mondo è breve sogno

> (the fruit of my raving is shame, and repentance,
> and the clear knowledge that what pleases in this
> world is a brief dream; 12–14).[38]

In the last canzone, he prays Mary to help him now that death is near, and repeats his confession of sin, error and repentance. The love story of the *Canzoniere* — a spiritual autobiography that describes, in a non-organic, not rigidly structured manner, the inner experiences of the poet — is divided into two major sections, one 'in vita' and one 'in morte' of Laura. The second section opens with canzone CCLXIV, where the author's divided mind between love for Laura and love for God is the central theme, issuing in a declaration of impotence: "et veggio 'l meglio, et al peggior m'appiglio" (I see the best, but hang on to the worst).[39] Though 'penitential' compositions are present in the first part of the *Canzoniere*[40] — thus showing that Petrarch's consciousness is fully

37. Further studies on the Middle English religious lyrics about the Virgin are presented by R. Woolf, *The English Religious Lyric in the Middle Ages* (Oxford, 1968), pp. 114–58 and 274–308; and D. Gray, *Themes and Images in the Medieval English Religious Lyric* (London–Boston, 1972), pp. 75–121.
38. I use G. Contini's edition of the *Canzoniere* (Turin, 1979 edn.).
39. Derived from Ovid, *Metamorphoses*, VII, 20–1.
40. For instance, LXII, *Padre del ciel*; LXXX, *Chi è fermato*; LXXXI, *Io son sí stanco*; CXLII, *A la dolce ombra*.

alert throughout the collection and that religious impulses are strong even at the point of maximum infatuation with Laura[41] – a decided turning point in this direction is represented by the last four poems of the second part. If, in sonnet CCCLXII, the poet's thought, flying to Heaven, prays God to be enabled to contemplate both His and transfigured Laura's face (11), in sonnet CCCLXIII Laura's death becomes the starting point of a return to God alone. Free from love (9–11) – and this freedom is both bitter and sweet – with thoughts now incapable of daring flights and feelings deprived of both warmth and coldness, hope and grief (6–8), tired of and sated with living, the poet turns to the Lord he now adores and thanks:

> Morte à spento quel sol ch'abagliar suolmi,
> e 'n tenebre son li occhi interi et saldi;
> terra è quella ond'io ebbi et freddi et caldi;
> spenti son i miei lauri, or querce et olmi:
> . . .
> et al Signor ch'i' adoro et ch'i' ringratio,
> che pur col ciglio il ciel governa et folce,
> torno stanco di viver, nonché satio.
> (1–4; 12–14)

The tiredness that dominates here, the sense of a soul exhausted and, as it were, both placated and expiring, recurs in sonnet CCCLXIV ("Omai son stanco", 5), but accompanied by a more active repentance. Reviewing the thirty-one years in which Love has kept him in the fire both during Laura's life and after her death (1–4), Petrarch reproaches himself for the "error" which has almost completely extinguished in him any "seed of virtue" (5–7) and devoutly "renders" his final years to God (7–8). He is now "pentito et tristo" of the years he has spent as he should not have (9–11) and implores the Lord who has imprisoned him in his earthly gaol to free him and save him from Hell, for he knows his fault and does not excuse it (12–14).

In sonnet CCCLXV the invocation to the "invisible, immortal King of Heaven" (6) is more pressing. It occupies three out of four stanzas, in which the poet, aware of his "mali" which have now become "indegni et empi", asks for help to his "frail and erring" soul and for the divine grace that can compensate its defects (5–8). If he has lived in war and storms, may he at least die in peace and

---

41. The fact that Petrarch organized the *Canzoniere* – that we do not have in it a mere chronological-autobiographical sequence, but a conscious artistic construction – indicates, moreover, that he deliberately chose to present himself in this manner. On the problem of the 'making' of the *Canzoniere*, see now K. Foster, *Petrarch: Poet and Humanist* (Edinburgh, 1984), pp. 92–105 and references therein.

"in porto" (9–11). And may God's hand help him in whatever life is left him, and in death (12–14). Once more, this prayer is preceded by a meditation on the past (1–4), on which Petrarch weeps now as he wasted it "in loving a mortal thing" instead of lifting himself up in flight though he had 'wings' for it:

> I' vo piangendo i miei passati tempi
> i quai posi in amar cosa mortale,
> *senza levarmi a volo, abbiend'io l'ale,*
> per dar forse di me non bassi exempi.
> (1–4)

Here, the image of flying and wings, which I have stressed in quoting the passage, is used in a way fundamentally different from Dante's. There, in *Paradiso* XXXIII, the need to ask for Mary's help was expressed as a *sine qua non:* whosoever wants grace and does not pray to her will "fly his desire without wings". Here, Petrarch states that he did indeed have wings to attain the highest Good and thus make of himself an "example", but he did not even attempt to fly. There, we see Dante in the supremely humble posture of one who has flown to the Heavens and implores for a final grace, the vision of God. Here, we see Petrarch regret never having left the earth and his love for "cosa mortale", Laura.

What, in other words, we witness in these sonnets is the gradual maturing of a conversion the seeds of which are present from much earlier on in the *Canzoniere*,[42] but which is precipitated by the growing awareness of death's imminence and a sense of tiredness and dissatisfaction with life. Detachment from Laura, even as transfigured after her death,[43] becomes repentance from past errors and finally rejection of love for "cosa mortale". Hence, Petrarch turns to God and asks for peace.

It is this intensely, personally lived summing up and coming to an end of a whole experience of feelings and sufferings that *Vergine bella* retraces. And it is significant that after repeatedly invoking God in the last sonnets, the poet should turn to Mary — like Dante before the very end of his poem — for an *elogium* as well as a *supplicatio*. When the symbolic year of man's life indicated by the number of poems in the *Canzoniere* (366 minus the Prologue sonnet)[44] comes to an end, Petrarch replaces Laura with the Virgin.[45]

---

42. And in *Secretum* III. See Foster, *Petrarch*, p. 42, on the relationship between *Canzoniere, Secretum* and *Triumphus Eternitatis*.
43. In the so-called 'apparition' poems, for which see Foster, *Petrarch*, pp. 80–7.
44. See Foster, p. 96 and pp. 198–9, n. 91 for references.
45. On the Mary-Laura contrast, see N. Iliescu, *Il Canzoniere petrarchesco e Sant'Agostino* (Rome, 1962), pp. 90–1; B. Martinelli, *Petrarca e il Ventoso* (Bari, 1977), pp. 225–39.

The construction of *Vergine bella* is highly elaborate. Carducci and Ferrari called it "both canzone and lauda, both hymn and elegy", and added that

> as hymn or lauda, it is objective and it sings the praises of the Virgin; as elegy or canzone, it is subjective and it describes the poet's feelings. Of the hymn, or Christian prayer and litany, it maintains the continuous invocation, 'Vergine', which is repeated at line 1 and line 9 of each stanza. It is a hymn especially in the first five stanzas (1–78): here, after the invocation and the proposition (1–8), come the prayers and the praises. The latter are mostly contained in the first eight lines of each stanza; in the following five, beginning with the apostrophe, 'Vergine', are contained the prayers – and these are general, that the Virgin may turn to him, obtain for him grace, peace, and good speed. In the second part, that is, in the last five stanzas and in the envoy (79–136), it is canzone and elegy. From line 79 to line 103 the poet confesses his vanity and earthly love, and prays to have rest to that passion which is still burning in him. In the remaining lines, he recommends himself, as a Christian and a devout person, that he may have mercy, contrition, and a good death.[46]

The first thing one notices in reading *Vergine bella* after Dante's prayer or even Chaucer's *ABC* is that figural images have totally disappeared. There are only two 'historical' references, one to Christ's Passion (22–4), and one to Eve, whose "pianto" the Virgin has turned into "allegrezza" (36). The central 'theological' image is of course that of the Incarnation, which is repeated, with variations, at least once in each of the first six stanzas (6, 28, 30–2, 43, 56–8, 76–9). Scriptural, dogmatic, and liturgical definitions are present throughout,[47] often employed with that "wit" which, according to Walter Ong, medieval writers use to describe the divine "mystery".[48] Thus, for instance, Mary is called "virgo sapiens, et una de numero prudentum" (14–16), "scutum" (17), and "refugium peccatorum" (20). In the third stanza, which I here take as an example, the echos of the liturgy and the play on mystery are as intense as in Dante. Petrarch begins by calling Mary "pure and intact Virgin", and immediately adds "noble daughter and mother of your issue", ending the invocation with the image of the Virgin as light of this world and ornament of Paradise. In the second section of the stanza Mary, now "fenestra coeli" (31), "benedicta inter mulieres" (35), called "beata" by all generations (38), and "crowned" in Heaven (39), is implored for her Son's grace (37). Her

46. F. Petrarca, *Le Rime*, ed. G. Carducci and S. Ferrari (Florence, 1978 edn.), p. 511.
47. For a complete survey of these, see the notes in Carducci-Ferrari, pp. 512–21.
48. W.J. Ong, "Wit and Mystery: A Revaluation in Medieval Latin Hymnody", *Speculum*, XXII (1947), 310–41.

Son, the Son of the highest Father (30), "verbum ipsum in extremis diebus, salutis nostrae causa, in utero ipsius habitavit" (32). "Ab aeterno ordinata" (34), chosen among all other women (33–4), she turned Eve's tears into joy (36):

> Vergine pura, d'ogni parte intera,
> del tuo parto gentil figliuola et madre,
> ch'allumi questa vita, et l'altra adorni,
> per te il tuo figlio, et quel del sommo Padre,
> o fenestra del ciel lucente altera,
> venne a salvarne in su li extremi giorni;
> et fra tutti terreni altri soggiorni
> sola tu fosti electa,
> Vergine benedetta,
> che 'l pianto d'Eva in allegrezza torni.
> Fammi, ché puoi, de la Sua gratia degno,
> senza fine o beata,
> già coronata nel superno regno.
> (27–39)

Here, reminiscences from the Gospels, the Church's antiphons, Venantius Fortunatus, St John of Damascus and Dante[49] are blended in an unique amalgam.

Elsewhere, what strikes the reader is the way in which the love images of the *Canzoniere* are applied in a totally religious sphere. When, opening the canzone, Petrarch calls Mary "beautiful virgin", "clothed with the sun", "crowned with stars", he clearly adapts images from the Song of Songs (1.7) and the Apocalypse (12.1), but we cannot forget that throughout the *Canzoniere* Laura is presented as a sun surrounded by stars. Nor can we neglect the fact that the "amor" which now prompts the poet to speak of the Virgin (4) and with which the Holy Ghost incarnated Himself in her womb (6) is a purely heavenly love, quite different from that which reigns elsewhere in the collection. Indeed, the very invocation for mercy here addressed to Mary is generally addressed to Laura, and the love and the faith towards Mary proclaimed in the first stanza (4, 8) are explicitly opposed to the faithful love for Laura recalled in the last (122).

This transformation of love language into the language of religion — a phenomenon which is common, and in both directions, throughout the Middle Ages — culminates, through a revisitation of the poet's own past life and an examination of his present condition, in a rejection of Laura. A triple series of images, which becomes more intense in the second part, dominates in

49. See Carducci-Ferrari, pp. 513–15.

Vergine bella. The first focusses on the poet's "error". The "cieco ardor" that "burns" among "stupid mortals" (20–1) is gradually transformed and finally seen as the poet's own "dubio stato" (25). The "secol pien d'errori oscuri et folti" (45) becomes a personal "fallo" (62), a "torta via" (65), an "error"(111), a "madness" (117). The "war" of the first stanza (12) recurs as the terrible storm in which the poet finds himself alone, "senza governo" (69–70), and as the "affanno" which is the epitome of his life (84).

Death – the second series of images – is more and more impending. Coupled with Fortune as the ruler of the world's affliction in the second stanza (18), it is again viewed as a very personal fact – the poet's own "ultime strida" (71), his "last year" (88), his approaching death (91). From "extremo passo" (107) to "ultimo pianto" (115), to the very last day (131) death obsesses the writer. "Conscience" and "death" do indeed "sting" him (134).

The images of 'earth' and 'earthliness' sum up this particular dimension. "Earth", as opposed to Mary's "Heaven", is the poet himself (13); "earth" is Laura now dead (92), and "poca mortal terra caduca" is even the Laura he loves with such wonderful faith (121). And he prays that his last tears may be devout, "without earthly smire" (115–16).

Gradually, through this triple movement, there emerges a rejection of Laura. At first this happens implicitly, as the poet calls Mary "*vera* beatrice" (52). Earlier on in the *Canzoniere*, Laura had twice been given that very attribute of 'bringer of happiness' (LXXII, 37; CXCI, 7). Nor should we, in our context, forget the way in which Dante's Beatrice is sublimated, left behind, and yet always present at the end of the *Divine Comedy*.[50]

Five stanzas later, the rejection of Laura is explicit. Petrarch now calls her "Medusa" and says that she and his error have made him a stone "dripping with vain tears" (111–12). As Medusa, she had been enchanting earlier in the collection (CLXXIX, 10 and CXCVII, 6), but as "a mere image of the love-obsession, almost without moral overtones".[51] Here she is seen, because of the poet's own 'error', as bewitching, with a decidedly moral implication. Hence, the writer now views his entire life as the obsessive pursuit of "mortal beauty, acts and words" (85–6). Stanza 7 is perhaps the most 'autobiographical' of

50. For this, and the Dantean overtones and implications of Petrarch's "beatrice", see K. Foster, "Beatrice or Medusa: the Penitential Element in Petrarch's 'Canzoniere' ", in C.P. Brand, K. Foster, U. Limentani, eds., *Italian Studies Presented to E.R. Vincent* (Cambridge, 1962), pp. 41–3.
51. Foster, "Beatrice or Medusa", pp. 52–3.

Vergine bella and the one where Petrarch's examination of conscience and final repentance vibrate with the most intense emotion:

> Vergine, quante lagrime ò già sparte,
> quante lusinghe et quanti preghi indarno,
> pur per mia pena et per mio grave danno!
> Da poi ch'i' nacqui in su la riva d'Arno,
> cercando or questa et or quel'altra parte,
> non è stata mia vita altro ch'affanno.
> Mortal bellezza, atti et parole m'ànno
> tutta ingombrata l'alma.
> Vergine sacra et alma,
> non tardar, ch'i' son forse a l'ultimo anno.
> I dí miei piú correnti che saetta
> fra miserie et peccati
> sonsen' andati, et sol Morte n'aspetta.
> (79–91)

The conversion prepared and asked for in the next two stanzas is so complete ("cangiati desiri", 130), that the poet declares that if he can leave his "stato assai misero et vile" with Mary's help (124–5; the verb he uses, "resurgo", has an obvious religious overtone), he will consecrate to her name his whole mind and art,

> et penseri e 'ngegno et stile,
> la lingua e 'l cor, le lagrime e i sospiri.
> (127–8)

Thus, with a 'retractation' which seems to be much more final than the one Chaucer apparently added at the end of the *Canterbury Tales*, Petrarch ends his poem. When, in the envoy, he asks the Virgin to recommend him to her Son, "true man and true God", that He may welcome his "spirto ultimo" "in peace' (135–7), we realize that we have gone through the whole of a man's experience, the whole of his "guerra" to be ready, with him, for ultimate "pace". The 'biographical' elements implicit in the image of Dante who has seen the "spiritual lives one by one", or in that of Deguileville's 'pilgrimage of the life of man', are here completely personalized. Dante's example is obviously present, even determining, in Petrarch's mind, to the point of making him conclude the *Canzoniere* with a Prayer to the Virgin after the 'Pater' of sonnet LXII and the implorations to God in sonnets CCCLXIV–V. But Petrarch's Prayer to the Virgin – and he must have invoked her often since in his will be mentions a picture of the Madonna he had at home and which he believed to be Giotto's work – is not, like Dante's, the prologue to a beatific vision,[52]

---

52. Petrarch's version of the beatific vision, *with* Laura now triumphing in the world after resurrection, will take place in what is the last poem he wrote, the *Triumphus Eternitatis*, for a comparison of which with *Vergine bella*, see Foster, "Beatrice or Medusa", pp. 53–5, and now his *Petrarch*, pp. 42–3.

nor merely, like the pilgrim's of Deguileville's poem, an imploration of help in a moment of crisis and temptation. It is a poet's searching review of his entire life, a surrendering of himself to God's hands,[53] a deliberate, artistic decision to end the *Canzoniere* with Buonconte da Montefeltro's last cry to Mary.

We have already seen how our fourth and latest author, Chaucer, transforms the Prayer to the Virgin inserted in a narrative context into a 'private' lyric. Chaucer's Marian 'poems' and his personal devotion to the Virgin must have been well known. In his *Regement of Princes*, Hoccleve mentions the "many lines" his "master" wrote in honour of Mary "wyth lovyng herte" and calls Chaucer the Virgin's "servaunt" (4985–91). Did Hoccleve know more 'lyrical' pieces by Chaucer on Mary than have come down to us? Or did he count the Prologues to the *Prioress's* and the *Second Nun's Tales* simply as "lines" in honour of the Virgin? In other words, would these, together with the *ABC*, be taken as lyrical Prayers, isolated from their narrative contexts? Now that we have studied Petrarch's *Vergine bella*, it will be enough to set Chaucer's *ABC* against it to see how 'impersonal' the English translation of Deguileville's Prayer is when compared to the intensely autobiographical poem that concludes the *Canzoniere*. What I propose to do now is to examine Chaucer's other Marian 'lyrics' not as such, but as parts of narratives – to study what happens to the Prayer to the Virgin when it is taken out of a narrative context to be employed in another narrative. For this is precisely what occurs, and on three different occasions, when Chaucer handles Dante's Prayer.

Let us begin, then, with *Troilus and Criseyde*.[54] Book III of the poem celebrates, after a splendid invocation-hymn to Venus by the poet, Troilus' supreme bliss – his conquest of Criseyde and the consummation of their love. In the course of this celebration, Troilus himself pronounces two hymns to Love, one during his night in Criseyde's bed, and one at the end of the Book in the presence of Pandarus. In the first (1254–74) he salutes Love, Venus and Imeneus (1254–60), who have "brought [him] fro cares colde", and then turns to Love himself:

53. Compare lines 135–7 of *Vergine bella* with Luke's "Pater, in manus tuas commendo spiritum meum" (23. 46).
54. I leave aside the problem of the chronology of Chaucer's poems. What interests me here is not in what order the *Troilus* and the Prologues to the *Prioress's* and the *Second Nun's Tales* were composed, but what use Chaucer makes in them of the Prayer to the Virgin such as he read in *Paradiso* XXXIII.

> "Benigne Love, thow holy bond of thynges,
> Whoso wol grace, and list the nought honouren,
> Lo, his desir wol fle withouten wynges.
> For noldestow of bownte hem socouren
> That serven best and most alwey labouren,
> Yet were al lost, that dar I wel seyn certes,
> But if thi grace passed oure desertes.
>
> And for thow me, that leest koude disserve
> Of hem that noumbred ben unto thi grace,
> Hast holpen, ther I likly was to sterve,
> And me bistowed in so heigh a place
> That thilke boundes may no blisse pace,
> I kan namore; but laude and reverence
> Be to thy bounte and thyn excellence!"
> (III, 1261—74)

The second and third line of the first stanza are a translation of lines 13—15 of Dante's Prayer to the Virgin:

> Donna, se' tanto grande e tanto vali,
> che qual vuol grazia e a te non ricorre
> sua disianza vuol volar sanz'ali.

Troilus is calling the God of Love the unique medium of grace as Dante and St Bernard had done with Mary. He is using a religious image of divine grace in a secular context. This is not, in itself, surprising in a medieval poem. But the shift of emphasis in these stanzas makes us pause. In the first, Troilus thanks Venus, Love and Hymen for having done *him* a service. In the third, he gives "laude and reverence" to the "bounte" and "excellence" of Love, who has granted *him* "grace", helped him as he "likly was to sterve", and allowed him to have the secular equivalent of a beatific vision, bestowing him "in so heigh a place / That thilke boundes may no blisse pace". In the second stanza, the meditation is more general: "*whoso* wol grace", "*hem* socouren", "*oure* desertes".

Now, what causes Troilus' *elogium* of Love is not the vision of Mary's triumph in the Empyrean, but the view, and the fondling of, and the delight in, a rather different "hevene":

> Hire armes smale, hire streghte bak and softe,
> Hire sydes longe, flesshly, smothe, and white
> He gan to stroke, and good thrift bad ful ofte
> Hire snowisshe throte, hire brestes rounde and lite:
> Thus in this hevene he gan hym to delite,
> And therwithal a thousand tyme hire kiste,
> That what to don, for joie unnethe he wiste.
> (III, 1247—53)

And at the end of his hymn Troilus does not direct his gaze into God, but kisses Criseyde again (1275–6). The contrast with Dante's experience seems deliberate, as the quotation from *Paradiso* XXXIII and the allusions to Heaven, grace, bliss, to the very passing from "cares colde" and death to the "heigh place" – from Inferno to Paradise – would indicate.

Yet there is in Troilus, as well as in his narrator, a complementary movement. Both celebrate here the sublimation of love as emotional and sexual experience in a kind of ecstasy, of supreme rapture (*raptus* was the word theologians used to describe Paul's vision of God in II Corinthians 12, and hence the necessary state a man must be in to obtain a beatific vision):

> For out of wo in blisse now they flete;
> (III, 1221)

But this experience acquires a higher status once Troilus starts meditating on it. When, in his hymn, he passes from his own concerns in the first stanza to general considerations in the second, the Love which he had already called "Charite" (1254) becomes "benigne Love" and above all "holy bond of thynges" (1261). The Narrator had anticipated this in his Prologue to the third Book, describing the universal power of the "blisful light", "of which the bemes clere/Adorneth al the thridde heven faire". God Himself, he said there, loves:

> In hevene and helle, in erthe and salte see
> Is felt thi myght, if that I wel descerne;
> As man, brid, best, fissh, herbe, and grene tree
> Thee fele in tymes with vapour eterne.
> God loveth, and to love wol nought werne;
> And in this world no lyves creature
> Withouten love is worth, or may endure.
> (III, 8–14)

The last three lines of this stanza, be it noted, have only a partial precedent in Boccaccio's original (*Filostrato*, III, 74–79), where the *gods* ("iddii", 74, 7) accompany men and the animal and vegetable kingdoms in 'feeling' the might of Venus, and where *God* as agent of love is totally absent. Troilus will return to this idea of cosmic love in his hymn at the end of Book III, which is totally detached from contingent concerns. There, the splendid Boethian mould of the four stanzas containing Troilus' song is Chaucer's closest equivalent to Dante's "amor che move il sole e l'altre stelle": [55]

---

55. See P. Dronke, "L'amor che move il sole e l'altre stelle", now in his *The Medieval Poet and his World* (Rome, 1984), pp. 439–75, and especially 470–5.

"Love, that of erthe and se hath governaunce,
Love, that his hestes hath in hevenes hye,
Love, that with an holsom alliaunce . . .
. . .
"So wolde God, that auctour is of kynde,
That with his bond Love of his vertu liste
To cerclen hertes alle, and faste bynde,
That from his bond no wight the wey out wiste . . ."
(III, 1744—68)

Troilus' use of some lines from St Bernard's Prayer to the Virgin responds, then, to the deeper logic of Chaucer's poem. It is part of a wider pattern in which human, sexual love is seen as a manifestation of the love that governs the whole universe. But it is also a double-edged image. Troilus may, in his meditation, come close to the world of the spirit — does indeed seem to fly "his desir" *with* "wynges" to the "grace" of the "holy bond of thynges" — but he begins by stroking Criseyde's body and ends by kissing her. His flight ultimately is "withouten wynges", for the object through which Troilus wants and seems to attain cosmic love is decidedly earthly.[56] Like Petrarch in his adoration of Laura, Troilus has forgotten love *for* God.[57] In this he is of course justified, as he is supposed to be, after all, a pagan, though one who mentions *God*.[58] But the narrator who extols Troilus' love and the cosmic might of Venus cannot adhere to 'oblivio Dei' for long. In the Prologue to Book III he declares, "God loveth, and to love wol nought werne", but this is only one side of the coin. "L'amor che move il sole e l'altre stelle", the last line of the *Divine Comedy*, is only the subject in a sentence where Dante's desire and will are the object. Like a wheel that is evenly moved, these are now revolved by the love which moves the sun and the other stars. Dante's desire and will become part of the same movement which involves the universe and which proceeds from God's love. This, however, is possible only because Dante's love for God has led him to conform to God's love for him and the world.[59] And I suspect that the reason why Chaucer does not use the last line of *Paradiso* **XXXIII** in the third Book of *Troilus* (in spite of the fact that it would apparently fit very well with Troilus' second hymn to Love and would come natural to a poet who had employed lines from that Canto earlier on) is precisely his awareness of the context in which that verse is inserted.

56. The best pages I know on this passage have been written by W. Wetherbee, *Chaucer and the Poets: An Essay on Troilus and Criseyde* (Ithaca and London, 1984), pp. 80—3 and 109—10.
57. Foster, *Petrarch*, pp. 74—5.
58. And see A. Minnis, *Chaucer and Pagan Antiquity* (Cambridge, 1982), pp. 61—107.
59. And see K. Foster, *The Two Dantes* (London, 1977), pp. 37—55.

For the author of *Troilus* knows very well what the place of love for God should be. At the end of his "litel bok", after paying homage to poetic tradition and placing himself within it, and after recommending that no one "myswrite" and "mysmetre" his poem (V, 1786–99), Chaucer relates his hero's death in a single stanza, which shows how un-Iliadic his book has been. The "wrath" of Troilus (a deliberate take-off of the *Iliad's* first line, which Chaucer knew from Latin "florilegia") is "despitously" abated by the "fierse Achille" (Achilles' 'wrath', indeed!) in one single line (1800–6). Then, following Boccaccio's Arcita,[60] Troilus' ghost ascends to the eighth sphere, where it contemplates the "erratik sterres, herkenyng armonye/With sownes ful of hevenyssh melodie" (1807–13). Immediately afterwards, the soul of the Trojan hero turns its gaze downwards, where he beholds "this litel spot of erthe" and consequently despises "this wrecched world" (1814–20).

This ascension corresponds to Dante's arrival into the *eighth* sphere when, prompted by Beatrice, he casts his eyes through the heavens he has passed and down to "this globe", now such, he says, that he smiled at its paltry semblance (*Paradiso*, XXII, 133–8, 139–53). It is Dante's last glance at Earth. In the following Canto, he witnesses the triumph of Christ and Mary which I discussed at the beginning of this essay.

Troilus, instead, looks intently at the spot where he was slain and laughs at the grief of those who weep over his death (1821–22). His soul had, a moment before, "held al vanite/To respect of the pleyn felicite/That is in hevene above". It now condemns

> . . . al oure werk that foloweth so
> The blynde lust, the which that may nat laste,
> And sholden al oure herte on heven caste.
> (V, 1823–5)

The great love of Book III has become but an aspect of the "*blynde* lust" which cannot last long though it dominates "oure werk".

Troilus' soul is spared further recantation. While realizing how "pleyn" is the happiness of the "hevene above", the immortal essence of Troilus proceeds, as Mercury guides it, to a dwelling which, like the Boccaccio of the *Teseida*, Chaucer leaves mysterious (1826–7). The Stoic end of Troilus is, however, insufficient for his creator. Speaking now in the first person, and prompted by Boccaccio (*Filostrato*, VIII, 28), he launches into a melancholy consideration of Troilus' love story:

60. *Teseida*, XI, 1–3, in turn following the *Somnium Scipionis* in *De re publica* I, 7, 11, and the ascent of Pompey's soul in Lucan's *Pharsalia*, IX, 1–18.

116

> Swich fyn hath, lo, this Troilus for love:
> . . .
> Swich fyn his lust . . .
> (V, 1828—31)

Then, once more following Boccaccio (*Filostrato*, VIII, 29, 1—5), but boldly abandoning his source after two lines, Chaucer appeals to the "yonge, fresshe folkes" "in which that love up groweth" and invites them to cast their hearts to that God who has made them in His image (1835—41). And it is here that the correspondence between the love of God for man and that which man ought to bear to God is finally preached in purely Christian terms and opposed to "feynede loves":

> And *loveth* hym, the which that right for *love*
> Upon a crois, oure soules for to beye,
> First starf, and roos, and sit in hevene above;
> For he nyl falsen no wight, dar I seye,
> That wol his herte al holly on hym leye.
> And syn he best to *love* is, and most meke,
> What nedeth *feynede loves* for to seke?
> (V, 1842—8)

Hence, the poet now looks with disdain at the "corsed olde rites" of pagans, the "wrecched appetites" of this world, the "fyn and guerdoun" one gains in serving the rabble of heathen deities, the "forme" itself "of olde clerkis speche/ In poetrie" (1849—55). Recommending his book to his friends Gower and Strode (1856—9), he turns "to that sothefast Crist" who, as he has just said and repeats here, died on the cross (1860, 1842—4) for *love*. With all his heart, he ends his poem, like Petrarch his *Canzoniere*, with a prayer — one to the Lord in the Trinity as celebrated by Dante in *Paradiso* XIV, but one in which the last line, with a final twist on the original, and repeating once more the word 'love', sends back to us an echo of the Prayer to the Virgin:[61]

> Thow oon, and two, and thre, eterne on lyve,
> That regnest ay in thre, and two, and oon,
> Uncircumscript, and al maist circumscrive,
> Us from visible and invisible foon
> Defende, and to thy mercy, everichon,

61. The first two lines are translated from *Paradiso*, XIV, 28—30. The last line asks mercy of Christ *for love* of His Mother. In Dante's prayer, Bernard asks Mary to help Dante see God. He calls her "Vergine madre" (1), recalls his love (7) and her benignity (16, the line after those Chaucer uses in *Troilus*, III, 1262—3). On the ending of *Troilus*, see my *English Medieval Narrative* (Cambridge, 1982), pp. 223—6; and Wetherbee, *Chaucer and the Poets*, pp. 224—43, who is unaware of what I said on this passage in *Chaucer and the Italian Trecento* (Cambridge, 1983), pp. 127—9.

> So make us, Jesus, for thi mercy digne,
> *For love of mayde and moder thyn benigne.*
> (V, 1863–9)

The way in which Dante's Prayer to the Virgin and the lines from *Paradiso* XIV are used in the *Troilus* corresponds, then, to a precise, 'ideal' as well as narrative, strategy. In Book III, a few lines from Dante's Marian eulogy are inserted into a paean that celebrates the power of sexual attraction and fulfilment as an aspect of cosmic Love. Though the use of sacred images in courtly poetry and viceversa is fairly common in the Middle Ages, here it reaches a startling climax. Yet the context in which this image is employed is somewhat ambiguous. And it is this ambiguity that the narrator brings out fully in his epilogue, where, again by means of Dante, he points to the importance, in a Christian civilization, of man-God and God-man love.

The other occasions on which Chaucer uses Dante's prayer to the Virgin are very different. In the Prologues to the Prioress's and the Second Nun's stories such as we read them in Fragments VII and VIII of the *Canterbury Tales*,[62] the Invocation to Mary has a more straighforward function. When, after the Shipman, the Prioress is invited to tell a tale, she begins by invoking the Lord[63] and talking about the way His name is celebrated by "men of dignitee" as well as by "the mouth of children" (453–9). It is, therefore, "in laude" of God and Mary that she will do her "labour" "to telle a storie" (460–6). At this point, the Prioress inserts her Prayer to the Virgin, which occupies three stanzas (467–87). The first two are an *elogium*, the third a *supplicatio*. But in the last line of the first and third stanzas the speaker invokes Mary's help in her narrative enterprise:

> Help me to telle it in thy reverence! (VII, 473)
> Gydeth my song that I shal of yow seye. (VII, 487)

The Prioress, then, announces the theme and the purpose of her tale, which is about and for Mary. The Virgin represents, however, the epitome of divine mystery, as the first stanza makes absolutely clear:

---

62. Here, I am not concerned with the problem of the composition of the *Canterbury Tales*, and in particular with whether the *Second Nun's Tale* was written for that collection or earlier and independently of it. For references, see Robinson's notes, pp. 734–5 and 756–7. It has also been suggested that Chaucer used in the Prioress's Prologue his own translation of Dante's Prayer such as we now read in the Prologue to the *Second Nun's Tale:* see R.A. Pratt, "Chaucer Borrowing from Himself", *Modern Language Quarterly*, VII (1946), 259–64.
63. The invocation is derived from Psalm 8. 1–2.

> O mooder Mayde! o mayde Mooder free!
> O bussh unbrent, brennynge in Moyses sighte,
> That ravyshedest doun fro the Deitee,
> Thurgh thyn humblesse, the Goost that in th'alighte,
> Of whos vertu, whan he thyn herte lighte,
> Conceyved was the Fadres sapience,
> Help me to telle it in thy reverence!
> (467–73)

Here, especially if compared to the *ABC*, the language is rich, compressed, figural as well as dogmatic. The Dantean lesson has been learnt to perfection.[64] And to Dante the Prioress turns in her second stanza, where the Virgin's virtues are celebrated in the inexpressibility topos (476), and prevenient grace is evoked (477–8) to recall precisely the function that the Prayer to the Virgin had in *Paradiso* XXXIII – that of obtaining, through Mary, the "lyght" by which man is guided unto her Son (479–80):

> Lady, thy bountee, thy magnificence,
> Thy vertu, and thy grete humylitee,
> Ther may no tonge expresse in no science;
> For somtyme, Lady, er men praye to thee,
> Thou goost biforn of thy benygnytee,
> And getest us the lyght, of thy preyere,
> To gyden us unto thy Sone so deere.
> (474–80)

In the final stanza of the Prologue the Prioress turns to her own lack of "konnyng" and incapacity to express herself:

> My konnyng is so wayk, o blisful Queene,
> For to declare thy grete worthynesse
> That I ne may the weighte nat susteene;
> But as a child of twelf month oold, or lesse,
> That kan unnethes any word expresse,
> Right so fare I, and therfore I yow preye,
> Gydeth my song that I shal of yow seye.
> (481–7)

Dante complains about this very incapacity three times in *Paradiso* XXXIII (55–7, 106–8, 121–3), and he once asks the "somma luce" to make his tongue so powerful that he may leave at least a spark of Its glory to people in the future (67–72). And the child imagery associated with the vision of the supreme mysteries (*Paradiso*, XXIII, 121–6, and XXX, 82–7) is here employed to describe Dante's "corta favella" before he plunges into the three gyres of the Trinity:

64. And see Kean, *Chaucer*, pp. 195–6.

Omai sarà piú corta mia favella,
pur a quel ch'io ricordo, che d'un fante
che bagni ancor la lingua a la mammella.
(XXXIII, 106–8)

It will not, therefore, seem farfetched to suggest that the idea of making his
Prioress illustrate her incapacity to express herself by way of the image of the
little child came to Chaucer's mind from Dante's supreme Canto, to be appropriately associated with the story of the Prioress's little boy. She, the teller,
is indeed like a baby, smaller even than her protagonist, and incapable of
words, whereas he, the little child of her tale, will sing, and in Latin, to the
greater glory of Mary and God.

The story that the Prioress proceeds to tell after this invocation is not a
beatific vision, but a miracle of the Virgin. But a literal comparison with
Dante's final Canto is misleading. The *Prioress's Tale* and the *Second Nun's
Tale* represent the only examples of religious narrative and the only two
celebrations of human love for God in a fully Christian sense in the *Canterbury Tales*. In these two stories, the human logic and motivations which rule
the world of the other tales seem to be suspended. Nor is the way chosen by
Chaucer to show how man can reach God negative, as happens in the *Parson's
Tale*, which purports to point out to the other pilgrims the way 'of thilke par-
fit glorious pilgrymage/That highte Jerusalem celestial" (X, 50–1) but does
so by means of a sermon on *penitence*. The Parson tells us what we should
not do and what we ought to repent of if we want to attain the heavenly
Jerusalem. The Prioress and the Second Nun tell us what some people are
capable of doing for love of God.

In both cases, this love culminates in martyrdom. Chaucer, who seems incapable of the philosophical and mystical *élan* necessary to a beatific vision and
who makes final his decision against it in the *House of Fame*,[65] is, like Petrarch, prepared to renounce human for divine love. He does so in the final
stanzas of *Troilus*. In the tales of the Prioress and the Second Nun, he goes
beyond this. Here, he does not simply pray. In the *Prioress's Tale* he recounts
the story of a child who, in love with Marian songs, is murdered and hidden
away by the Jews of his town. When his mother, a widow also devoted to
Mary, looks for him in the Jewish ghetto, the child, though "with throte ykorven", starts singing *Alma redemptoris*. While the Jews are killed in an awful

65. *House of Fame*, 972–92; and see my *Chaucer and the Imaginary World of Fame*
(Cambridge, 1984), pp. 197–8.

pogrom, the child is brought on a bier before the high altar and, blessed with holy water, once more sings the Marian antiphon. The abbot then asks him to explain why he can sing though his throat has been cut. And the child explains that the law of nature (650) is suspended in him because Jesus "wil that his glorie laste and be in mynde" (653).

But it is his devotion to Mary — that very devotion with which the Prioress had invoked the Virgin in her Prologue — that has produced the miracle, as the child himself declares:

> "This welle of mercy, Cristes mooder sweete,
> I loved alwey, as after my konnynge;
> And whan that I my lyf sholde forlete,
> To me she cam, and bad me for to synge
> This anthem verraily in my deyynge,
> As ye han herd, and whan that I hadde songe,
> Me thoughte she leyde a greyn upon my tonge.
> "Wherfore I synge, and synge moot certeyn,
> In honour of that blisful Mayden free,
> Til fro my tonge of taken is the greyn;
> And after that thus seyde she to me:
> 'My litel child, now wol I fecche thee,
> Whan that the greyn is fro thy tonge ytake.
> Be nat agast, I wol thee nat forsake.'"
> (656–69)

The logic of these two stanzas corresponds to that of the Prioress's Prologue, down to the "konnynge" of the second line, which recalls the "konnyng" of line 481.

The *exemplum* of Chaucer's "litel clergeon" is an extreme. He is a seven-year old who is taught devotion to Mary (505–12) and learns the first verse of *Alma redemptoris* though he does not understand Latin (523–4). He asks an older boy to explain the meaning to him, then learns all of it off by heart, and sings it on his way to school and back. The portrait we have of him in the Prioress's words centres on his simplicity, single-minded determination, devotion, and innocence.[66] He illustrates perfectly Jesus' preaching in the Gospel:

> And Jesus called a little child unto him, and set him in the midst of them, and said, Verily I say unto you, Except ye be converted, and become as little children, ye shall not enter into the kingdom of heaven. Whosoever therefore shall humble himself as this little child,

66. He is called "innocent" three times (538, 566, 635) and celebrated as one of the Innocents at line 608. And see Robinson's notes to 579 ff. and 627, p. 735, and references therein.

the same is the greatest in the kingdom of heaven. And whoso shall
receive one such little child in my name receiveth me.[67]
(Matthew 18. 2–5)

And indeed the human punishment of the Jewish murderers does not simply
respond to the *lex talionis* proclaimed by the provost, "Yvele shal have that
yvele wol deserve" (632),[68] but also to the warning Jesus gives to those who
harm his 'parvuli':

> But whoso shall offend one of these little ones which believe in me,
> it were better for him that a millstone were hanged about his neck,
> and that he were drowned in the depth of the sea.
> (Matthew 18. 6)

The Prioress's little child 'is' Christ in the same manner as the little child received in Jesus' name 'is' Jesus in the Gospel. And the *Tale* widens and deep-
ens this dimension by making its protagonist appear as an heir of Abel, one
of the Holy Innocents of Herod's massacre, a follower of the Lamb,[69] a
St Nicholas (513–15), and a Hugh of Lincoln (684–5). From Genesis to the
Gospels, to the Apocalypse and to saints' legends, Chaucer's 'parvulus' is
innocence and martyrdom, in and out of time. The subject of the *Prioress's
Tale* might seem less exalted than Dante's beatific vision, but it is absolutely
central to Christianity, for it is no less than the condition itself upon which
man can gain entrance into the kingdom of heaven visited by Dante and
closed to the jeweller of *Pearl* and the pilgrim of Deguileville: "Except ye be
converted, and become as little children, ye shall not enter into the *kingdom
of heaven*". It is therefore appropriate that its teller should invoke Mary's help
in a high-sounding Prayer to the Virgin, and its audience be left marvellously
"sobre" at the end (691–2).

Similarly, if not more appropriate, is the 'Invocacio ad Mariam' in the Second
Nun's Prologue. Here, the speaker is particularly close to Dante, whose St
Bernard is evoked in the second line of the Invocation (30) and whose *elo-
gium* is adapted fairly faithfully:[70]

67. Cf. Mark 10. 13–16.
68. For which see Robinson's note, p. 736.
69. Line 578 is a reminiscence of Genesis 4.10 (where God reproaches Cain for the
murder of Abel); in line 574 the Jews are called "cursed folk of Herodes al newe",
and the "innocentz" are celebrated in line 608. The episode of the massacre is recalled at line 627, where the child's mother is seen as "newe Rachel" with an echo
of Matthew 2. 18 (itself a figural use of Jeremiah 31.15). The image of the Lamb
taken from Apocalypse 14. 3–5 is elaborated upon in lines 579–85 (for which see
Robinson's references in note to 579 ff., p. 735).
70. The best comparative examination of the two passages is now to be found in H.
Schless, *Chaucer and Dante: A Revaluation* (Norman, Oklahoma, 1984), pp. 214–17.
See also R.A. Peck, "The Ideas of 'Entente' and Translation in Chaucer's *Second
Nun's Tale*", *Annuale Mediaevale*, VIII (1967), 17–37.

Thow Mayde and Mooder, doghter of thy Sone,
Thow welle of mercy, synful soules cure,
In whom that God for bountee chees to wone,
Thow humble, and heigh over every creature,
Thow nobledest so ferforth oure nature,
That no desdeyn the Makere hadde of kynde
His Sone in blood and flessh to clothe and wynde.

Withinne the cloistre blisful of thy sydis
Took mannes shap the eterneel love and pees,
That of the tryne compas lord and gyde is,
Whom erthe and see and hevene, out of relees,
Ay heryen; and thou, Virgine wemmelees,
Baar of thy body — and dweltest mayden pure —
The Creatour of every creature.

Assembled is in thee magnificence
With mercy, goodnesse, and with swich pitee
That thou, that art the sonne of excellence
Nat oonly helpest hem that preyen thee,
But often tyme, of thy benygnytee,
Ful frely, er that men thyn help biseche,
Thou goost biforn, and art hir lyves leche.

(36–56)

Once more, the comparison with Chaucer's own *ABC* shows how Dante's model prompts the English author to treat the eulogy in a highly rhetorical manner, interweaving sources[71] and images and producing a compact lyrical piece. As examples, I would point to at least two sets of lines. In the first, Chaucer takes Dante's

> Tu se' colei che l'umana natura
> nobilitasti sí che 'l suo fattore
> non disdegnò di farsi sua fattura,

and, translating the first line and a half, enlarges on the rest, rendering "fattore" with "the Makere ... of kynde" and loosening "fattura" into "his Sone in blood and flessh to clothe and wynde". Thus, Dante's 'audacia' is lessened and made plain, and a new rhetorical pattern is found. The concept is taken up again in the following stanza, where the mystery of the Incarnation is dwelt upon at greater length and inserted into a cosmic background (43–7), the paradox of maternity in virginity being repeated together with that of the "Creatour of every creature" borne by a human "body" (47–9).

---

71. On these, see Robinson, pp. 756–7.

123

In the second set of lines, Chaucer keeps an eye on Dante, but alters the ideas and their sequence, integrating them with images taken from elsewhere. Thus, "nel ventre tuo" is amplified into "withinne the cloistre blisful of thy sydis" by the introduction of the traditional 'claustrum' image. "Raccese", which in Dante represents the first image of fire and warmth and which implies a revival of God's love for man after the Fall, is replaced by the much plainer "took mannes shap". The "germinating flower" of Dante's ninth line is eliminated. "Amore" and "etterna pace" are kept, but not in Dante's highly elaborate sequence, where "amore" means God's love and the Holy Ghost as subject, and "etterna pace" indicates the place where the protagonist now finds himself – the Empyrean – as well as the 'aeterna pax' to which all beings tend with their desire (*Paradiso*, III, 85–7). In Chaucer, "the eterneel love and pees" are, together, the cumulative subject of the Incarnation, of "took mannes shap". They are God, whose power is described in the following line, "that of the tryne compas lord and gyde is". Here, "tryne compas" means the threefold world of earth, sea and heaven evoked immediately afterwards, but the suggestion of the triple circle of the Trinity such as described by Dante towards the end of *Paradiso* XXXIII may also be present.[72] In any case, the image seems to suggest a reflection in the tripartite nature of the visible universe of the trinitarian nature of the Deity.

In other words, what we have in the first four stanzas of the 'Invocacio ad Mariam' is a solemn evocation of the supreme mysteries in the form of an *elogium*. The *supplicatio* comes in the next three stanzas (57–77), where the speaker asks Mary for mercy and help as a human being steeped in sin (58, 62, 71–4) and as the singer of St Cecilia's life. In fact, consideration for the task of 'enditing' a sacred subject opens and closes the 'Invocacio' (29–35 and 78–84). At the beginning, inspiration is asked of Mary as the Muse of this particular tale. At the end, the humility formula sends the audience back to the source, Jacopo da Varazze's *Legenda Aurea*. The composition and telling of the story are given a theological justification. As "feith", says the narrator, "is deed withouten werkis", "wit and space" "for to werken" are implored of Mary so as to obtain salvation from Hell (64–6). But the 'work' the

72. In this case the "eterneel love and pees" (i.e., God, called both "Amor" and "Pax" by for instance Pseudo-Dionysius in *De Divinis Nominibus*, IV, lectio IX, 160; e IV, lectio XVII, 207) would be "lord and gyde" of the Trinity – a concept which would be theologically daring. Robinson, p. 757, quotes a hymn by Venantius Fortunatus in which the "trina machina" is the threefold universe.

speaker means is not just the 'opera' in general without which, as James' Epistle proclaims (2. 17 and 20), "fides ... mortua est in semet ipsa" – it clearly is the narrator's present "werk" (77 and 84).

The *Second Nun's Tale* is presented to us, then, as the religious opposite of *Troilus and Criseyde.* Mary replaces the Muses and the Furies. The author appeals to his authority's "wordes and sentence", and trusts his "werk" to the audience's "amende". In Book III of *Troilus*, as we have seen, Venus and Love are celebrated as the supreme powers of earth, sea, and heaven (8 and 1744– 5). In the Prologue to the *Second Nun's Tale* "erthe and see and hevene" "ay heryen" the "eterneel love and pees", God, the true "lord and gyde" of "the tryne compas". A straight line seems to link the Epilogue of *Troilus*, with its Dantean prayer to the Trinity and the love of the Virgin Mother, to the Dantean Prologue to the *Second Nun's Tale.* Nor is it perhaps without significance that in neither the Prioress's nor the Second Nun's Prologues do we find any trace of Troilus' perversion of the Dantean "sua disianza vuol volar sanz'ali". It looks as if, having given Dante's "disianza" the erotic connotation of "desir" in the *Troilus*, Chaucer decided to avoid this image in a 'sacred' context. Though on both occasions he translates the *terzina* that immediately follows those two lines (*Paradiso*, XXXIII, 16–18; *Prioress's Tale*, 477–8; *Second Nun's Tale*, 52–6), reproducing the concept of prevenient grace, he eliminates the splendid 'flying without wings' which is the epitome of Troilus' adventure in life *and* death (whilst the not flying, though he had wings, was viewed by Petrarch as the epitome of his life).

That the enterprise to which Chaucer is now setting hand in the *Second Nun's Tale* is intended to be a great one is confirmed also by his reproduction of the "Interpretacio nominis Cecilie quam ponuit Frater Jacobus Januensis in Legenda". The fivefold etymology of 'Cecilia' makes the protagonist of the story a mirror of Heaven on earth and an intermediary between them. Cecilia is "hevenes lilie" but also "the wey to blynde". She is "hevene" and "Lia", that is, "in figurynge", "thoght of hoolynesse" and active life. She is "wantynge of blyndnesse" "for hir grete light / Of sapience, and for hire thewes clere". She is, finally, "hevene" and "leos", "the hevene of peple", "ensample of goode and wise werkes alle" (85–105). In the last two stanzas of the 'Interpretacio', Chaucer enlarges upon his source and alters its conceptual sequence[73] to make the name of the saint acquire a cosmic and celestial dimension (107–8, 114–15).

---

73. Compare Jacopo's text in W.F. Bryan and G. Dempster, eds., *Sources and Analogues of Chaucer's Canterbury Tales* (Chicago, 1941), p. 671.

Cecilia, already the epitome of "chastnesse of virginitee", "honestee", "conscience", "goode fame", "good techynge", the contemplative and active lives, "sapience" and "goode and wise werkes", becomes now "of feith the magnanymyte", "the cleernesse hool of sapience", and "sondry werkes, brighte of excellence". Thus, *spiritualiter* ("goostly"), she is the heaven in which the sun, the moon and the stars are visible (106–12). And like heaven, she has roundness and wholeness, the swiftness in movement of the Primum Mobile, and the "brennynge", the *ardor* of the Empyrean (113–18).[74]

The "lyf of Seinte Cecile" *is*, then, a beatific vision *sui generis*,[75] appropriately prefaced by a Prayer to the Virgin. Chaucer not only loved the intense lyricism of the Dantean eulogy, but also understood its narrative, poetic, and theological function. For what follows in the tale is, as in the Prioress's, an extreme story of devotion to Christ and to the ideal of chastity and 'maydenhede'. Cecilia is going to be married to Valerian. She does not refuse marriage, but asks that she may keep virginity in it – a totally 'unnatural' request, which hardly agrees with the Church's matrimonial doctrine. But the laws of nature are suspended in this tale as they are in the Prioress's, and to an even greater extent. Here, the supernatural is present not only in the miracle of Cecilia surviving and preaching for three days though "with hir nekke ykorven" – as the Prioress's little child sings "with throte ykorven" – but also in the various visions that mark the most important stages of the story and point to the ultimate vision of God.

When Cecilia tells her husband she has an angel for lover and entreats him to "gye" her "in clene love", she adds that if he will do so, the angel will show him "his joye and his brightnesse" (161). Later, when Valerian, until now "a fiers leoun", becomes a "lomb" before Pope Urban, an old man "clad in white clothes cleere" and with "a book with lettre of gold in honde" appears to him. This 'senex', so similar to Dante's St Bernard, is none other than St Paul who, instead of showing truth and pointing to Death in a 'negative' parable like the Old Man of the *Pardoner's Tale*, announces the mystery of God *aureis litteris:*

> Unus Dominus, una fides, unum baptisma. Unus Deus et pater omnium, qui est super omnes et per omnia et in omnibus nobis. (Ephesians 4. 5–6)

74. See Robinson, p. 757, note to 114.
75. In her *The Structure of the Canterbury Tales* (London, 1983), Helen Cooper maintains that Chaucer's "work barely touches on such ultimate religious experience as the beatific vision (the *Second Nun's Tale* comes closest)", p. 72. Cooper's statement and her examination later of the *Second Nun's Tale* (pp. 188–95) are among the best I have read on the subject, and in what follows I am deeply indebted to her analysis.

O Lord, o feith, o God, withouten mo,
O Cristendom, and Fader of alle also,
Aboven alle and over alle everywhere.
(207–9)

And as soon as the newly christened Valerian arrives at home, he sees Cecilia's angel with two crowns, of roses and lilies (symbols of martyrdom and purity),[76] which he says he has brought "fro paradys" and will never rot or lose their perfurme. Valerian's brother, Tiburce, smells this scent when he reaches the couple but cannot see the crowns. The "swete smel" operates in him a wonderful metamorphosis: "hath chaunged me al in another kynde" (252). Cecilia leads the two men "to blisse above" (281), as before the angel had promised her and Valerian the "palm of martirdom" and participation into God's "blisful feste" (240–1).

Truth, then, is what man beholds when he is ready for conversion. When Tiburce asks Valerian whether what he has said about the existence of the two crowns was "in soothnesse" or heard "in dreem", Valerian answers with a phrase that announces a total revolution of natural law:

"In dremes", quod Valerian, "han we be
Unto this tyme, brother myn, ywis.
But now at erst in trouthe oure dwellyng is".
(262–4)

In truth, be it noted, not 'in reality'. For this 'truth' is the subject of Paul's Epistle to the Ephesians, where the Apostle advocates "the perfecting of the saints", "the work of the ministry", "the edifying of the body of Christ", "till we all come in the unity of the faith, and of the knowledge of the Son of God, unto a perfect man, unto the measure of the stature of the fulness of Christ" and, "speaking the truth in love, may grow up into him in all things, which is the head, even Christ" (4. 12–15). Putting off the "old man" and putting on the "new man" (4. 22–24), the Christian must not walk "as other Gentiles walk, in the vanity of their mind, having the understanding darkened, being alienated from the life of God through the ignorance that is in them, because of the blindness of their heart" (4. 17–18).

The story of Cecilia, Valerian and Tiburce is an illustration of these words. Cecilia shows Tiburce, and will later tell Almachius, that "alle ydoles nys but a thyng in veyn" — that the heathen, gentile religion is dumb and deaf, the pagan gods but stones, and whoever believes in them is blind (284–91, 498–

---

76. For this, see Robinson's note to 220 ff., p. 758.

511). The *Second Nun's Tale* brings to completion Chaucer's detachment from the "payens corsed olde rites", from the "rascaille" of Jove, Apollo and Mars announced at the end of *Troilus*. It makes man's love for Christ finally correspond to Christ's love for man.[77] In the *Troilus* epilogue, as we have seen, the narrator invites the "yonge, fresshe folkes" to love Him, "the which that right for love/Upon a crois, oure soules for to beye,/First starf, and roos, and sit in hevene above". But Cecilia's whole life is devoted to this love — "for his love that dyde upon a tree" (138) — and her "lover" is an angel, as the initially and understandably incredulous Tiburce, threatening her with a truly Sicilian 'delitto d'onore', must come to realize.

Hence, the 'truth' of the *Second Nun's Tale* is that of life after death, of the Trinity, of the Redemption, which Cecilia expounds to Tiburce (320–48). The ultimate truth is the "corone of lif that may nat faille" which will receive the martyrs after death, their souls reaching the "Kyng of grace" — Maximus' vision of their ascent, their "gliding" to Heaven "with aungels ful of cleernesse and of light" (402–3).

The itinerary of Valerian, Tiburce and Maximus thus faithfully reproduces an 'itinerarium perfectionis' of conversion, martyrdom, and elevation to God's presence. The "cleernesse" and the "light" of Maximus' vision are the nearest Chaucer comes to Dante's beatific vision, and the closest to it he is prepared to take us in the *Canterbury Tales*.

The action of St Paul's Christian people "speaking the truth in love" does however also have a paramount 'earthly' consequence. Initiated by Cecilia and then pursued by Valerian, Tiburce, Maximus, and other "ministres" of Almachius (410–20), this is the spreading of Christianity through martyrdom, the gradual building of the primitive Church in history. And it is precisely this "augmentum corporis ... in aedificationem sui in caritate" (Ephesians 4. 16), this growth of the *ecclesia*, that Cecilia fittingly wants to have commemorated "perpetuelly" after her death by the building of a church (545–6). Her house becomes the Church of St Cecilia in Rome,

> In which, into this day, in noble wyse,
> Men doon to Crist and to his seint servyse.

77. It might, then, be possible to conclude that the "lyf of Seint Cecile" stems from the same kind of inspiration that inspired the epilogue of *Troilus*. Are the two contemporary? The image of Chaucer that emerges from a comparison between the pagan and secular poet on the one hand and that of the religious writer on the other may suggest something like 'The Two Chaucers' as the title of yet another book on 'him'.

It is, amongst the various messages of the *Canterbury Tales*, one we tend to forget. But, whenever the *Second Nun's Tale* became part of that collection of stories, it was clearly meant to take its place with the *Prioress's Tale* in an ideal pair of hagiographic visions of central Christian truths, as Petrarch's 'penitential' sonnets and *Vergine bella* are meant to have a special position in the *Canzoniere*.

The movement which started in *Troilus* now comes to completion. The presence of Dante's *Paradiso* and in particular of his Prayer to the Virgin accompanies its salient stages. Thus, to study the forms and functions of the *Invocacio ad Mariam* in Dante, Deguileville, Petrarch and Chaucer means to observe not only fundamental changes in genre and style — from narrative to lyric back to narrative, from fiction to autobiography to allegory and back to fiction; from the Bernardine amalgam of figural, dogmatic, historical, and emotional elements to a more personal, intimate emphasis and back to Dante's rhetoric as revisited by Chaucer — but also different approaches to religion. In Dante, the *elogium* is the prologue to a beatific vision: it brings him back to Mary before plunging him into God. Later, the *supplicatio* becomes an invocation in the crises of human life and a private prayer 'in hora mortis nostrae', celebration and rejection of human love, prologue to a miracle and a story of martyrdom in a collection of tales told on a fictitious pilgrimage. To understand all this, it may be enough to recall John Donne's lines on the Annunciation:

> Thou hast light in dark; and shutt'st in little room,
> *Immensity cloistered in thy dear womb.*

The Story-Teller and His Audience:
The Legend of Good Women

Dieter Mehl

Chaucer's first collection of stories, the *Legend of Good Women*, was evidently written between *Troilus and Criseyde* and the *Canterbury Tales* because it
explicitly refers to the Trojan epic and is in turn quoted in the prologue to
the "Man of Law's Tale". Of all the narrative poems it is probably the least
popular although it is by no means less original, but shows us Chaucer in as
experimental and exploratory a mood as any of the others. Many accounts of
the *Legend* start from an openly apologetic position or begin with the admis-
sion that this is indeed an inferior and uncharacteristically conventional work.[1]
It is not entirely Chaucer's fault, however, that we have lost the taste for brief
and fairly unadorned narrative or that we find the provocative reinterpreta-
tion of classical stories, whose original versions we are no longer familiar with,
less exciting than Chaucer and many of his contemporaries must have done.
Twelve manuscripts preserve the *Legend of Good Women* or parts of it, almost as many as the *Parliament of Fowls* and four times as many as the *Book
of the Duchess* and the *House of Fame*. "Comparisons are odorous", as
Shakespeare's Dogberry knew, and there is nothing to be gained by demon-
strating that the *Legend of Good Women* is inferior to the *Canterbury Tales*.
It will certainly never enjoy anything like the same popularity, but then it
does not claim to be the same kind of story-collection and its appeal is more
limited by its very subject and, perhaps, by its confessedly more literary character. Form and subject-matter suggest that Chaucer was consciously attempt-
ing something beyond the scope of his earlier work, a decisive extension of
the concept of courtly love (if indeed this is still the right term) and a choice
of material that invites comparison with the famous poets of Rome and Italy.

---

1. One of the first and most thorough modern accounts of the collection and its prob-
lems is R.W. Frank, Jr., *Chaucer and* The Legend of Good Women (Cambridge, Mass.,
1972). He sees the *Legend* as an important stage in Chaucer's development as a storyteller between *Troilus* and the *Canterbury Tales*.

The Prologue

Viewed superficially, the prologue once more harks back to the earlier love-visions, but it is even more personal and free from the restraints imposed by the traditional genre. The legends themselves are for the most part based on Ovid, that is, they take their subjects from pagan antiquity and whatever "modern" issue they are meant to illustrate, they do so in a deliberately detached and generalizing manner. The same applies, of course, to *Troilus and Criseyde*, but the *Legend* goes a step further by the variety of stories and the greater number of characters, all of whom have this in common: "And yit they were hethene, al the pak" (G, 299), as the God of Love says, choosing a rather provocative colloquial turn of phrase. If we look at the nine tales in the light of what Chaucer had attempted and achieved before he started on this collection, we are in a better position to appreciate their originality and their experimental qualities. Not only did Chaucer succeed in introducing a wealth of new material to English literature by opening up the rich storehouse of Ovidian mythology, with its inexhaustible variety of character and incident; this also presented him with the challenge of an undogmatic diversity of male and female characters who would not fit into the traditional roles of courtly love-literature. He had to find new ways of drawing such unexpected and unpredictable figures, in situations not to be found in his earlier poetry. In this he may not have been quite as successful as in many of the *Canterbury Tales*, but if we compare the *Legend* with any of the earlier narratives, including even *Troilus and Criseyde*, we are bound to see a definite advance in scope and variety, even though the subject does not allow for unlimited freedom of stylistic experiment.

What makes the prologue so different from the earlier dream-visions is the way in which the new subject is introduced. Even more distinctly than in the *Parliament of Fowls* or the *House of Fame*, the narrator sees himself and is seen by others, not as an unsuccessful lover, but as a poet with a respectable number of works to his credit. In fact, the prologue contains the earliest bibliography of Chaucer and a particularly valuable one at that because it lists some titles we would otherwise know nothing of, like "the Wreched Engendrynge of Mankynde" (G, 414) and "Orygenes upon the Maudeleyne" (G, 418). It cannot be ruled out, of course, that these are only fake titles, but it is more likely that the works are lost. In any case, the list is impressive enough and it is clear that the real subject of the prologue is Chaucer's reputation as a poet and, in particular, the critical reception of his works.[2]

2. On the poetological aspects of the collection see the interesting study by L.J. Kiser, *Telling Classical Tales: Chaucer and the* Legend of Good Women (Ithaca, 1983).

The prologue begins with a wonderful account of the true function of literature and the indispensable contribution of books to our whole culture. One of the most important services of written texts is that they can tell us about things we have not seen ourselves and thus widen our knowledge beyond the scope and the possibilities of our own experience:

> A thousand sythes have I herd men telle
> That there is joye in hevene and peyne in helle,
> And I acorde wel that it be so;
> But natheles, this wot I wel also,
> That there ne is non that dwelleth in this contre,
> That eyther hath in helle or hevene ybe,
> Ne may of it non other weyes witen,
> But as he hath herd seyd or founde it writen;
> For by assay there may no man it preve.
> But Goddes forbode, but men shulde leve
> Wel more thyng than men han seyn with ye!
> Men shal nat wenen every thyng a lye,
> For that he say it nat of yore ago.
> God wot, a thyng is nevere the lesse so,
> Thow every wyght ne may it nat yse.
> (G, 1–15)

Chaucer goes beyond his earlier poems in his emphatic claim that there are things we will never see with our own eyes and in whose existence we should nevertheless believe because the poets testify to their reality. Truth is much wider than our own experience and literature acts as a kind of collective memory preserving the knowledge and thus even the reality of a whole world of facts and ideas that would otherwise be lost irretrievably:

> Thanne mote we to bokes that we fynde,
> Thourgh whiche that olde thynges ben in mynde,
> And to the doctryne of these olde wyse
> Yeven credence, in every skylful wyse,
> And trowen on these olde aproved storyes
> Of holynesse, of regnes, of victoryes,
> Of love, of hate, of othere sondry thynges,
> Of which I may nat make rehersynges.
> And if that olde bokes weren aweye,
> Yloren were of remembrance the keye.
> Wel oughte us thanne on olde bokes leve,
> There as there is non other assay by preve.
> (G, 17–28)

The examples mentioned by Chaucer (21–4) are the subjects of all kinds of narrative literature, be it saints' legends, history or romance, but perhaps the most significant item is the one mentioned in the very first lines of the poem, "hevene or helle". Nobody has ever been there and yet everybody believes in the existence of Heaven and Hell. This may be a pointed tribute to Dante's *Divina Commedia* whose narrator does indeed claim to have visited Hell and Heaven, if only in a divinely inspired poetic vision.[3] Whatever the realistic basis of his experience, we have no doubt about its truth and validity. At the same time, this may be one of Chaucer's modest disclaimers: his own subject is so much less lofty and yet the stories he is going to tell also have the truth and reality which is attested by books. The narrator's passion for reading is cheerfully admitted and not, as in earlier poems, presented in a slightly comical light as an inability to cope with the demands of actual experience.

The narrator goes on to confess — and this is a surprising change of direction — that there is one area of experience that makes even him forsake his books, and this is the season of spring, with its renewal of nature and the budding of flowers. The worship of May is here presented as a lively activity, placed in sharp contrast to the world of books:

> Farewel my bok, and my devocioun!
> (F, 39)

The (presumably later) G-version is a little less sweeping and suggests that the poet's devotion to books is interrupted just for this particular season:[4]

> Farwel my stodye, as lastynge that sesoun!
> (G, 39)

Of course, the traditional month of May, the month of love, is in a way as literary an experience as the books are; it can certainly not be regarded as an instance of real life versus books. After all, as every reader of Chaucer knows, the springtide with all its traditional paraphernalia is a literary convention as far removed from actual reality as many other subjects we read about, and at the same time just as near to some deeper levels of experience. Any reader will perceive that the object of the poet's delight, the daisy, is not some particular flower but an image of Love, of whole-hearted devotion to virtue and

3. See P. Boitani, "What Dante Meant to Chaucer", in P. Boitani (ed.), *Chaucer and the Italien Trecento* (Cambridge, 1983), pp. 115–39, especially pp. 125–6.
4. The differences between the two versions of the prologue are very interesting. See, for instance, D.S. Brewer, *Chaucer*, 3rd edn., (London, 1973), pp. 98–102. On the textual situation see the illuminating article by G. Kane, "The Text of *The Legend of Good Women* in CUL MS Gg. 4. 27", in D. Gray and E.G. Stanley (eds.), *Middle English Studies Presented to Norman Davis in Honour of his Seventieth Birthday* (Oxford, 1983), pp. 39–58.

honour and of the poet's wish to praise it with all the rhetorical gifts at his command.[5] Even after he has left his books, the narrator immediately returns to 'iterary considerations and to his own poetical efforts. His references to other poets and to the courtly party-game of the Flower and the Leaf must have meant more to his contemporary audience than it can possibly mean to us, but it is still evident that he is talking about his own position as a love-poet in this courtly society and wants to introduce his own stories, taken from old books, as a subject of at least equal relevance and authority as the new-fangled conventions of love-poetry.

In the later version (G), the poet goes to bed after roaming the meadows and he has a dream that is the subject of the rest of the prologue. He wakes up in the last two lines and begins to write the legends. The earlier version (F) has over a hundred lines more, mainly devoted to daisy-worship, and this makes the transition a little more awkward as well as perhaps overdoing the conventional praise of love, although I am not at all sure that this should be taken as a straightforward parody of courtly love. It may be deliberately conventional to contrast it with the highly original and personal sequel. The narrator's idea of love is clearly a limited one, not really informed with an experience of life's unpredictable variety, and there is something curiously artificial about his going to rest as if the conventional sleep, usually introduced at this point of a dream-vision, were deliberately staged:[6]

> Hom to myn hous ful swiftly I me spedde,
> And in a lytel herber that I have,
> Ybenched newe with turves, fresshe ygrave,
> I bad men shulde me my couche make;
> For deynte of the newe someres sake,
> I bad hem strowe floures on my bed.
> (G, 96–101)

This sounds almost like Orsino's self-indulgent devotion to love:

> Away before me to sweet beds of flowers!
> Love-thoughts lie rich when canopied with bowers.
> (*Twelfth Night*, I. 1. 41–2)

5. For a more sophisticated interpretation see the chapter "Daisies, the Sun, and Poetry", in Kiser, *Telling Classical Tales*, pp. 28–49.
6. In the F-version, the poet-narrator is himself more personally involved in the service of the Flower and the Leaf and he celebrates the worship of love. The G-version keeps the narrator more in the background or at least makes it clear that he is not a practitioner of love, but of love-poetry. It is more in keeping with the general theme of the prologue to make most of the poet's experience part of the dream. His life outside the dream is relevant to the reader only insofar as the narrator has produced translations and poetry on the subject of love.

It is, at any rate, quite different from the introductions to the earlier dream-visions where sleep comes far more naturally to the narrator. We have heard so much about the importance and the truth of books that we begin to look for vestiges of literary source-material everywhere. The narrator behaves as if he had read some of the more conventional dream-visions, like the *Book of the Duchess*, and this literary aspect is underlined by the subject of the dream itself. It begins, unremarkably enough, with the joy of the birds who happily remember St Valentine's Day, almost like an echo of the *Parliament of Fowls*, but it is not long before the God of Love is announced, and he is rather different from any of the allegories of the earlier poem. He is a bad-tempered monarch who is more respected for his imperious manner than for any true authority. Nor does he offer any conventional instruction, and his appearance or that of his followers hardly conform to the clichés of courtly love. The "Balade" sung by the ladies in praise of the Queen anticipates the subject of the stories the poet will be condemned to compose and its refrain is a superlative praise of Alceste whose "trouthe" in love puts all other heroines to shame. The concept of love is not defined, as usually, by the idea of faithful service and ennobling devotion, but by woman's loyalty and innocent suffering. The narrator is treated in a far less pleasant and more condescending manner than in any of his previous dreams. Instead of being rewarded for his naive interest in the subject he is turned away as "my mortal fo" (G, 248) and his most distinguished love-poetry is held against him as heresy and a disservice to love's cause.

Again, Chaucer has created a highly individual and teasingly ambiguous self-portrait. It is tempting, but in view of our limited knowledge unprofitable, to speculate whether there was in fact any official displeasure Chaucer wanted to answer or whether the whole situation is pure fiction. The poem creates its own reality, and we shall never know just what degree of actual experience and critical discussion are behind this passage. What makes it so interesting for us is the frankness with which Chaucer enters into a public debate on the subject of his own poetry and its reception. It soon becomes clear that Chaucer's most critical reader, the God of Love, is at the same time the most biased. This God of Love is not to be taken as a serious personification of a divine principle, but rather as a form of criticism of simple models of love-religion and outworn allegorical clichés. He is not only a rather haughty and self-important character, but also a remarkably unsystematic and narrow-minded literary critic.[7] Through prejudice or obtuseness he misunderstands

7. See the chapter "On Misunderstanding Texts", in Kiser, *Telling Classical Tales*, pp. 71–94.

the poet's intentions completely, which is emphasized by the fact that he picks out two of Chaucer's works that are the most unlikely witnesses for his alleged hostility to women. The *Roman de la Rose* can hardly be described as a work against women and love and in *Troilus and Criseyde*, Chaucer goes out of his way to soften the reader's predictable verdict on Criseyde and to present her as an object of pity. It is therefore not very likely that Chaucer himself would have agreed with Cupid's criticism; it makes more sense to assume that the God of Love is meant to represent a particular, limited and deplorably superficial reaction to Chaucer's poetry. He does not seem to know that at least some of the books he mentions to support his case contain some notorious anti-feminist satire and ironically undermine his argument.

The defence Chaucer puts up for himself as well as the Queen's apology on his behalf are interesting contributions to the discussion of the poet's purpose although neither is answered by the God of Love, who pardons the poet only to show his royal mercy and because of the Queen's intercession. To her he leaves the final verdict and the choice of the penalty and it becomes clear that the whole prologue has led up to this task imposed on the narrator. The stories introduced by this prologue are thus announced as a literary labour not undertaken voluntarily by the poet, but as an atonement for his earlier work. This raises a number of questions about the tone and the purpose of this collection, and the answers we give to them will largely determine our reaction to the legends.

If early readers had expressed their disapproval of Chaucer's portrayal of women, as the God of Love's attack seems to suggest, they must have found fault with the whole concept of courtly love. Their ideal of womanly behaviour, like that implied by Cupid, must have been concerned more with truth and constant relationships than with the lover's woe and his lady's pity. The modern reader may well ask which view is the more complimentary and there is no reason why Chaucer and his contemporaries should not have asked the same question. Cupid's account of virtuous women puts the finger on whole areas of experience which were simply not the subject of courtly love-poetry, but rather of saints' legends, except that he is explicitly referring to heathen ladies whose virtue is not grounded in holiness, but is presented as a natural female quality. Cupid is not interested in women as the objects of some lovers' devotion alone, but in all aspects of their relation to men. There are for him, as for many traditional moralists, three states, each with its proper code of behaviour:

> How clene maydenes, and how trewe wyves,
> How stedefaste widewes durynge alle here lyves,
> (G, 282–3)

This is repeated a few lines later:

> For alle keped they here maydenhede,
> Or elles wedlok, or here widewehede.
> (G, 294–5)

In other words, this Cupid is not the conventional God of Love at all, but the patron of steadfast women. For a modern feminist, this appears a severe limitation because women are defined only in their relation to marriage or rather to the opposite sex in general, but before we see this as a deliberate criticism on Chaucer's part we must first recognize that it is at least a considerable extension of love-poetry.[8] It is, of course, true that woman's role in medieval society was far more varied and included many activities outside marriage, but this is not really the point here because love-poetry does not claim to present the full range of human existence: it largely excludes the realities of professional and of domestic life. This applies to the lover as well as to the beloved, except that fighting is included in the knight's legitimate pursuits. But apart from vaguely described off-stage fights, Chaucer's Troilus, to mention but one instance, is hardly less "limited" than Criseyde. It is only his role as a lover the poet is concerned with, and it would be quite irrelevant to point out all the aspects of his personality the poem is silent about.

It seems equally beside the mark to fasten on the restrictive aspects of the prologue and to read an anti-feminist bias into its portrait of women. Within the context of traditional literary ideas about women, Cupid's praise of them is unexceptional. At least they are presented here in more than one capacity and more than one age-group. To praise their steadfast purity and "trouthe" is to give them credit for moral qualities and firmness of character rather than for beauty, attractiveness and the passive virtue of pity or the power to ennoble their lovers. This is certainly not in itself an antifeminist point of view. On the other hand, there is something in the tone of the dialogue that suggests that the God's line of argument is not taken entirely seriously by the poet himself, even though the narrator is forced into submission and agrees to the penalty with as good a grace as he can manage. The flaw in the ideal

---

8. See the interesting if somewhat biased article by E.T. Hansen, "Irony and the Anti-feminist Narrator in Chaucer's *Legend of Good Women*", *JEGP*, 82 (1983), 11–31.

picture presented by the God of Love is not that it comes short of the full range of women's activities or that it is too patronizing, but rather that it is too simple and too good to be true. To praise women in such fulsome and wholesale manner is hardly more adequate than to denounce them *in toto*, especially when the eulogy includes a sweeping disparagement of men. Coming from a man, this might well make the reader pause and wonder whether he is expected to take Cupid's account as the full story. What the dispute does, at any rate, is to announce a complete change of subject. To celebrate faithful women and their martyrdom is to turn away from love-poetry in the traditional sense and to try out new material. At the same time there is at least a suspicion that this could lead to a monotonous string of predictable biographies. The poet is told more than once that there is an inexhaustible number of women whose exemplary lives are worthy of being told, and at one point the Queen even suggests that he should devote all the remainder of his days to this task:

> Thow shalt, whil that thow livest, yer by yere,
> The moste partye of thy tyme spende
> In makynge of a gloryous legende
> Of goode women, maydenes and wyves,
> That were trewe in lovynge al here lyves;
> (G, 471–5)

When Chaucer or one of his characters is as emphatic as this it is usually a signal for the reader to be on his guard, and he surely does not misread the text if he begins to wonder whether the subject dictated to the poet is as rewarding as he is told. The narrator writes his stories under compulsion; it would have created quite a different impression if he himself had offered this collection as a voluntary penance, but though "thy penaunce is but lyte" (G, 485), the word "penaunce" rather suggests that the idea did not come from the poet himself and that we are therefore invited to question this choice of subject. It would be a gross simplification to say that the ideal of woman's truth and constancy is ridiculed, but it seems just as inadequate to take the poem entirely at its face value and thus to miss the irony of the title.

Above all, the choice of this particular narrative genre implies a rather limited view of the function of literature. Alceste and the God of Love evidently want to turn the narrator into a narrowly didactic poet, and their idea of the real moral impact of fictional narrative seems so much less complex and sophisticated than Chaucer's own. This is also emphasized by the God of Love's injunction to be brief:"Sey shortly" (F, 577). Brevity may be the soul of wit, but in medieval literature very short tales are, as a rule, simple *exempla* and it is doubtful whether Chaucer really felt that he could do justice to Ovid's complex stories when he turns them into brief summaries.

The collection is introduced as a secular legendary and we shall see how some of the stories had to be distorted in order to fit into this rigid scheme. Not every woman who died because of some man is necessarily a martyr and indiscriminate denunciation of women — even if the poet had been guilty of it — cannot effectively be answered by equally sweeping glorification.[9] Thus, the stories that follow are placed at a distance from the reader by the idea of penance as well as by the hesitation and humility of the narrator. We are deliberately encouraged to read them as a performance and this should make us more critically alert than we would be without this very personal introduction. As in Chaucer's early poems and, even more, in the *Canterbury Tales*, this provocative ambiguity of the narrative point of view is more important than any specific conclusions the individual reader may draw from it. The poet, out of genuine modesty or a sophisticated detachment, withholds any authorial interpretation or he presents it in such a way that it cannot possibly be taken literally.

Modern readers are at first inclined to suspect that Chaucer must have found these stories boring and that he gave up after nine legends to go on to the more exciting collection of the *Canterbury Tales*; but this is certainly wrong or at least much too simple. The importance of these legends lay first of all in the choice of classical stories, gleaned mainly from Ovid and various other authors or perhaps selections from classical writers, and in the adaptation of the material to a new kind of brief tale, complete in itself and yet part of a larger structure. Many or most were inspired by Ovid's *Heroides*, brief versions of classical stories, told from a personal and therefore distinctly limited angle. This makes for irony and doubt about traditional interpretations. Chaucer's treatment, similarly, suggests that there is more than one way of looking at time-honoured episodes and more than one possible judgement. The tone of the stories and especially the narrator's personal interventions discourage a naive and literal reading. Chaucer obviously delights in distancing stories by having them told in an ostensibly personal manner.[10] The narrator

9. The term "legend" is in itself rather ambiguous, because before Chaucer it was always restricted to saints' lives, not to unhappy lovers.
10. Kiser's description of the legendary as "self consciously 'bad art'" (p. 97) is, perhaps, a little too extreme, but her reading seems to me more in tune with Chaucer's intention than that of Frank.

takes sides vigorously and, according to the theme of his collection, acts the part of an uncritical defender of defenceless women. Excessive pity easily turns into condescension and the heroines are often reduced to rather marrowless objects of tearful commiseration. In the case of such powerful and politically or domestically active women as Cleopatra, Dido, and Medea this is particularly striking, and it is most improbable that Chaucer should not have been conscious of this consistent effect. It would be a distortion to call the narrator anti-feminist, but it is also clear that he is woman's friend only in a very narrow and biased sense and any reader who knows some of the original stories will notice the omissions.[11] Woman's role is mostly reduced to her relationship with some seductive man whom she is not able to hold as Criseyde held Troilus. Men are neither ennobled by women's company nor attracted by anything but their outward charm and quick submission. If the *Legend of Good Women* was read to an audience of women it is doubtful whether they can have been particularly flattered; it seems much more likely that Chaucer aimed at a more sophisticated effect. Any lady of half of Criseyde's quick intelligence might have resented this kind of pathetic appreciation until she saw the larger purpose of the collection and discovered some of its deeper ironies. It is obvious that the narrator is a *persona* created by the author and that we have to read the legends as a very personal statement. This is not meant in a strictly psychological sense and I think it is idle to speculate whether this narrator knows what he is doing or whether he is completely serious. His personal character is not really an issue here; at least it is far more important to recognize the discrepancy between the simple voice of the narrator and the sophistication of the whole collection. The narrator is not flatly discredited, but most readers will, after a while, feel a little superior to him and believe that they can see more in the text and the story-material than he himself does. This is precisely the effect Chaucer tries to achieve; at least this seems to me the most convincing explanation of the elusive style of the prologue and the legends.

The 'Legends'

The first legend, of Cleopatra, is a good example. It is, as far as we know, the first treatment of Cleopatra's story in English and if Chaucer had Boccaccio's account in *De Claris Mulieribus* (supplemented by the life of Antony in *De*

11. On this point see Hansen's article, quoted in note 8.

Casibus Virorum Illustrium) before him, which is very likely, he cannot have
been unaware of the fact that he was reinterpreting the character of Cleopatra completely.[12] Boccaccio is extremely hostile and though there were
more favourable versions of her story it is still obvious that Chaucer deliberately turned her into a pathetic martyr. It has often been remarked that
Chaucer opens his series of legends with a most unlikely candidate, but this
can hardly have been done unintentionally. The reader is once more reminded of the fact that this collection was not undertaken voluntarily and that the
author may have his own ideas about what he is sentenced to do. If the God
of Love was ignorant enough to offer "Jerome agayns Jovynyan" (G, 281)
as an authority on the perfection of women he might also fail to notice that
Cleopatra, whose story he explicity wants to come first, had a far from exemplary career. Or, to put it another way, the poet knows that stories can
create a new reality in its own right, a reality that can be very far from the
historical truth and yet valid and convincing in itself. Cleopatra is a particularly interesting instance of the poet's power to recreate a character, to trans-
form a crafty and notorious seductress into an innocent martyr. The vigorous
and disproportionately extended description of the sea-battle, which has
often puzzled critics, may be another sly pointer to the narrator's rather different interests and his admitted reluctance to perform the penitential task.[13]
Chaucer the poet stands at some distance from his narrator, encouraging the
reader to do the same.

Even if he was not making subtle fun of his penitential labour — and the question has to be decided by every reader for himself — he was certainly making
a provocative statement about the nature of "storyal soth" (G, 702), the
truth of literary tradition and the authority of written evidence. As he asserts
in the prologue, we all have to take many things on trust which we only
know from reading about them. Might not the same be true of Cleopatra and
the other women whose lives the poet is going to describe? Who knows what
the "real" Cleopatra was like? And if the God of Love wants to hear stories
of exemplary women, why not mould any famous biography into the prescribed form? It is certainly a very new concept of "storyal soth", but one
that — far from turning the *Legend* into a huge joke — raises fundamental
questions and opens an intriguing discussion on the nature and function of

12. See P. Godman, "Chaucer and Boccaccio's Latin Works", in P. Boitani (ed.), *Chaucer and the Italian Trecento*, pp. 269–95; on Cleopatra, pp. 281–90.
13. See Hansen, pp. 26–7.

poetry. The "Legend of Cleopatra" may be read as a demonstration of poetic fairness, of the poet's ability to wring pathos even out of the story of a royal whore, or of the independent authority of a poet's personal vision. In any case, it seems a far from inappropriate beginning of a series of legends, as long as we recognize that Chaucer was not just naively reproducing an old story. Cleopatra's "infinite variety" is reduced to pitiful weakness and simple truth to her "wyfhod": "Was nevere unto hire love a trewer quene" (G, 695). It is perfectly consistent and in keeping with Cupid's demand, as long as we do not remember that the original story was quite different. Are we meant to be deceived or should we notice the provocative discrepancy? The poet, I think, leaves the decision to the reader, but he knows what he knows.

Cleopatra's death is more theatrical than in any previous version of the story and it is possible to see it within an iconographic and homiletic tradition that adds another dimension to her character:

> Cleopatra in her death dramatizes, and accepts with a fiercely stoic courage, the medieval commonplace that man's flesh was eaten by worms and serpents in the grave.[14]

For "those who wish to respond to Chaucer's narrative most fully", this makes the legend of Cleopatra even more remarkable, and it may well be that Chaucer had the final, apparently never written legend of Alceste in mind, another, less gloomy comment on death and decay. In the present state of our knowledge and of the text it is difficult to judge what Chaucer ultimately meant by this impressively original version of Cleopatra's demonstrative end. There is nothing courtly about her love; it is only her suffering and "trouthe" the poet seems to be interested in and he holds her up as an example to men who habitually swear that they will die if their love is angry, but never do so. Cleopatra's death is thus presented as the opposite to merely rhetorical postures, but even here we cannot be absolutely certain of the narrator's sincerity and seriousness:

> But herkeneth, ye that speken of kyndenesse,
> Ye men that falsly sweren many an oth
> That ye wol deye, if that youre love be wroth,
> Here may ye sen of wemen which a trouthe!
> (F, 665–8)

14. See the excellent article by V.A. Kolve, "From Cleopatra to Alceste: An Iconographic Study of *The Legend of Good Women*", in J.P. Hermann and J.J. Burke, Jr. (eds.), *Signs and Symbols in Chaucer's Poetry* (Alabama, 1981), pp. 130–78. Quotations from p. 146 and 132.
Kiser sees the snake pit as an image of hell and points to the remarkable analogies between Cleopatra's legend and hagiographic traditions (pp. 107–9).

142

Is he really speaking from his heart or is he just paying lip-service to the God of Love's doctrine? Is Cleopatra's love of such high value that her sacrifice is justified? If she is criticized at all it is only indirectly, by the implied contrast to her "real" story and by the narrator's fulsome praise. This does not, however, question the ideal of "trouthe" or invalidate the story's claim that even a pagan woman can demonstrate some of the highest virtues and serve as a model for all lovers.

The "Legend of Thisbe" retells another well-known classical story, one of the most popular episodes from Ovid's *Metamorphoses* and one that, on the face of it, is much better suited to the poet's purpose in hand. Ovid's version is a model of concise and effective narration and Chaucer, following him pretty closely, must have realized that here was an author from whom he could learn a great deal; even by simple translation he could perfect his own mastery of the art of brief narrative, and Robert Frank, who gives a helpful account of the two versions, is quite right to insist on the importance and novelty of such compressed story-telling.[15]

Chaucer does not really reinterpret the old plot, but he introduces a number of small yet significant changes that, taken together, alter the tone and the emphasis of the original considerably. At first sight, Chaucer's legend seems to be nothing but a particularly successful and close translation, preserving the proportions and many brilliant details of the Latin text. There are hardly any substantial additions or surprising alterations, only a noticeable difference in vocabulary and style. It is perhaps inevitable that Chaucer's account of the lovers and their environment should suggest an English town rather than an exotic distant past. More important is the general effect of the relaxed and often colloquial tone that makes it much easier for the reader to enter into the story and to sympathize with these young people. The narrator even adds a little word of explanation when he feels he is relating something his audience might find strange. This creates a link between the poet and his readers and introduces an element of everyday experience and familiar reality which is important for our reaction to the story:

> For in that contre yit, withouten doute,
> Maydenes been ykept, for jelosye,
> Ful streyte, lest they diden som folye.
> (F, 721–3)

---

15. Frank, pp. 48–53. Kiser offers a more sophisticated reading and sees the "Legend of Thisbe" as an act of rebellion against the God of Love's demands. Chaucer's purpose is not very clear; the story is certainly not told as a straightforward parody, but it is more than an uncritical translation.

This is emphasized by the addition of some simple popular wisdom, evidently confirmed by the events of the tale — another appeal to our common knowledge of the world:

> As, wry the glede, and hotter is the fyr;
> Forbede a love, and it is ten so wod.
> (F, 735—6)

This reminds us a little of the style of *Troilus and Criseyde* except that love is portrayed here in far plainer and less sophisticated terms. There is no courtly ritual of falling in love or of extended wooing, but a straightforward process of mutual desire and uncomplicated purpose:

> Unto this clyft, as it was wont to be,
> Com Piramus, and after com Thysbe,
> And plyghten trouthe fully in here fey
> That ilke same nyght to stele awey,
> And to begile here wardeyns everichon,
> And forth out of the cite for to goon;
> (F, 776—81)

This directness is indeed new in Chaucer's love-poetry. He has not made the slightest attempt to turn Pyramus and Thisbe into courtly lovers and this marks an important step towards the unconventional diversity of the *Canterbury Tales*.

Chaucer evidently wants to colour Ovid's tale in such a way that it fits into his scheme and becomes the legend of a good woman. This is why early in the story he draws our attention to Thisbe's "trouthe" as to the most important motive of her actions. She is almost presented as the innocent victim of a moral ideal that can only be upheld at the expense of the lady:

> For alle hire frendes — for to save hire trouthe —
> She hath forsake; allas! and that is routhe
> That evere woman wolde ben so trewe
> To truste man, but she the bet hym knewe!
> (F, 798—801)

The tragic ending, too, is in Chaucer's version, a demonstration of Thisbe's "trouthe". Pyramus is not directly blamed for his part in the catastrophe, but he blames himself (as he does in Ovid) for asking the girl to meet him in such a dangerous place and it is clear that Thisbe is the real heroine. Her death is the climax of the story and it is described by her as proof of a woman's ability to be as faithful as any lover:

> But God forbede but a woman can
> Ben as trewe in lovynge as a man!
> And for my part, I shal anon it kythe."
> (F, 910–12)

By her suicide she is united with Pyramus, even without Ovid's final apotheosis, and the narrator draws the moral, confirming Thisbe's exemplary "trouthe" and women's equality to men in this respect. He does not omit to mention, however, that Pyramus too, unlike most of the male lovers in this collection, is "trewe and kynde" and that this is pleasing to "us men". This is a pointed reminder of the fact that the *Legend of Good Women* was composed by a man who is forced to admit, more or less grudgingly, that women are generally superior to men when it comes to "trouthe" in love. We are not allowed to forget that these stories, quite apart from their intrinsic value, are also a personal statement and must be read in the context of this particular narrative situation:

> And thus are Tisbe and Piramus ygo.
> Of trewe men I fynde but fewe mo
> In alle my bokes, save this Piramus,
> And therfore have I spoken of hym thus.
> For it is deynte to us men to fynde
> A man that can in love been trewe and kynde.
> Here may ye se, what lovere so he be,
> A woman dar and can as wel as he.
> (F, 916–23)

There is no marked contradiction between this conclusion and the original story; it is not a case of an established reading being turned upside down, as in the legend of Cleopatra, but we are, surely, allowed to wonder whether the events of the tale necessarily support the narrator's presentation of it as the legend of a martyr of love. At least Chaucer's friend Gower interpreted the lovers' tragedy in a very different way,[16] and the personal tone of Chaucer's version may be understood as an invitation to the reader to draw his own conclusions. The narrator's attitude to the story has to be seen in relation to his penance and to the royal command, but it is not the only possible interpretation and not an authoritative statement by Chaucer the poet, but rather a challenge to our own imagination and judgement. In this respect, the legend of Thisbe is not so very different from that of Cleopatra. The narrator's seemingly naive and literal obedience to the wishes of Alceste would strike us as

16. See Gower's *Confessio Amantis*, III, 1331–1494.

provokingly simple-minded were it not for some clear signs of the author's own sceptical detachment. He never, by subversive irony or implied criticism, flatly contradicts the moral of his stories as stated by the narrator, but he injects into his account enough teasingly controversial detail to make a perfectly simple reading unsatisfactory. As always in Chaucer, a good deal is left to the audience and this is not just an easy way out for the critic reluctant to commit himself, but an essential aspect of his art, an art that, above all, goes much deeper than "simpleminded moral clarity".[17]

This applies, in varying degrees, to all the other legends. Some of them give surprising versions of well-known stories, like the legend of Dido or of Medea, others seem more like faithful translations or deal with less familiar material. In some cases, the story did not have to be radically altered to make it fit into the general scheme of the collection, but in all of them we are reminded, explicitly or by implication, of the narrator who is doing his best to pile instance upon instance of betrayed women and treacherous men. There are several places where he lays it on so thick that even the God of Love might have found it a little too much of a good thing. A striking example is the double legend of Hypsipyle and Medea. It begins with a vigorous denunciation of Jason who seduced and forsook not just one woman but two:

> Thow rote of false lovers, Duc Jasoun,
> Thow sly devourere and confusioun
> Of gentil wemen, tendre creatures,
> Thow madest thy recleymyng and thy lures
> To ladyes of thy statly aparaunce,
> And of thy wordes, farced with plesaunce,
> And of thy feyned trouthe and thy manere,
> With thyn obeÿsaunce and humble cheere,
> And with thy contrefeted peyne and wo.
> There othere falsen oon, thow falsest two!
> (F, 1368–77)

Jason sounds like a parody of the courtly lover in the *Book of the Duchess* or a sinister version of Troilus. The main purpose of the legend seems to be the unmasking of such a villain:

> O, often swore thow that thow woldest dye
> For love, whan thow ne feltest maladye
> Save foul delyt, which that thow callest love!

17. See Kiser, who rightly claims that it is "unlike Chaucer to approve of any simpleminded moral clarity (such as that which the "good'women" are all meant to project)", p. 94.

146

> Yif that I live, thy name shal be shove
> In English that thy sekte shal be knowe!
> Have at thee, Jason! now thyn horn is blowe!
> (F, 1378–83)

Obviously, Jason's great sins are false swearing and "foul delyt", but the poet omits to mention the heroic feats of his famous expedition and he deliberately reduces a most colourful, complicated and justly celebrated story to a simple tale of betrayed love. In the sources, both Hypsipyle and Medea are far more spirited and interesting women. Medea, in particular, is the worst possible candidate for the pathetic legend of a guiltless martyr, and her awesome career does not by any stretch of the imagination confirm Cupid's or Alceste's views on the innocence of women. Chaucer offers a pointedly tendentious reading that flies in the face of most previous accounts and again makes us suspect that the poet and his narrator are greatly at variance here. One need not be a twentieth-century feminist to react to the story as one modern critic does:

> the juxtaposition of two women so easily taken in by one man makes it seem, again, common and inevitable that men betray and women beg for more.[18]

The long introduction to Hypsipyle's story, rather irrelevant to the ostensible purpose of the legend, suggests that the narrator is aware of the true nature of Jason's exploits and checks himself just in time before giving a too favourable picture. When he comes to the actual betrayal he only relates the barest facts and even hints that he does not want to give any encouragement to false lovers among his audience (F, 1554–8). The excessive brevity turns Hypsipyle into a completely insignificant figure; it is difficult to feel any sympathy for a character who is so easily taken in by a most transparent plot. Most of the wooing is done by proxy and there is no attempt to make her "fall" credible. All the narrator does, after the briefest of summaries, is to add an outline of Hypsipyle's letter from Ovid's *Heroides*, but there is no real attempt to make the most of the pathos of the situation or to arouse the reader's compassion.

Medea's story is given equally short shrift. Jason "That is of love devourer and dragoun" (F, 1581) is turned into a kind of Don Juan whose chief inter-

18. See Hansen, p. 26. Hansen is more concerned with the content, feminist or antifeminist, of the stories. Just as important, however, is the literary issue, the questioning of primitively didactic story-telling and stupid moralizing. In Ovid's *Heroides*, the two letters to Jason, by Hypsipyle and Medea, are separated by five other letters and in no way connected.

est is the seducing of women, and Medea falls for him within ten lines. Her colourful career as a sorceress is reduced to "the sleyghte of hire enchauntement" (F, 1650) and the gruesome murder of Jason's wife and children (Medea's own children) is omitted altogether. "It is difficult not to think Chaucer had his tongue in his cheek as he scratched away at Medea's story", says Robert Frank and he comes to the conclusion that Chaucer has failed to create a convincing unity of tone.[19] Whether the legend is a "failure" or not must be decided by every reader for himself, but it is important to recognize that deliberate violence has been done to a well-known story to bring it in line with the professed design of the whole collection. Whatever the poet's intention may have been, there is rather too much summary here and not enough dramatic narration to make the characters come alive, and the reader cannot be deeply involved in a story of which he is only given a bare outline.

The "Legend of Dido" is a far more successful abridgement although it is again a very one-sided version of a classical story. Chaucer was not the first to condemn Vergil's hero Aeneas and to make us see the whole episode from Dido's point of view. It had already been done, though in a very different way, in Ovid's *Heroides*, one of Chaucer's chief sources. Chaucer claims to follow Vergil's account as closely as space will permit him, but he is obviously more interested in the pathos of Dido's situation than in Aeneas' great mission as founder of Rome. He does not, however, reduce the story to a simple instance of betrayed love, but brings out the specific character and atmosphere of the whole situation and there is, at least in the first part, a strong sense that this love is the result of exceptional circumstances. Dido's pity for Aeneas' unprecedented suffering is a sign of her noble character and is carefully prepared by the way the hero is presented from her point of view (F, 1061–81). Of all the heroines of the *Legend of Good Women*, she is presented with most sympathy, without any admixture of patronizing sentimentality:

> Anon hire herte hath pite of his wo,
> And with that pite love com in also;
> And thus, for pite and for gentillesse,
> Refreshed moste he been of his distresse.
> (F, 1078–81)

Aeneas, too, is described in such a way that we can enter into his state of mind. After what he has gone through, the reception is so overwhelming that it is no wonder he becomes more than susceptible to his hostess' charm:

19. Frank, p. 84; he thinks the legend a failure (p. 90).

> He nevere beter at ese was in his lyve.
> Ful was the feste of deyntees and rychesse,
> Of instruments, of song, and of gladnesse,
> Of many an amorous lokyng and devys.
> This Eneas is come to paradys
> Out of the swolow of helle, and thus in joye
> Remembreth hym of his estat in Troye.
> (F, 1099–1105)[20]

It is Dido, though, who falls in love first and is tormented by this new passion; thus she seems to be doubly a victim to a power nobody can resist and victim to a "fals lovere" (F, 1236). There is no suggestion that Aeneas is really in love; he only takes what he can get. It is a complete reversal of the conventional wooing (F, 1192), whereas Aeneas only goes through the motions of protesting his love and promising eternal faith. The narrator interrupts the story to make his own position clear:

> O sely wemen, ful of innocence,
> Ful of pite, of trouthe, and conscience,
> What maketh yow to men to truste so?
> Have ye swych routhe upon hyre feyned wo,
> And han swich olde ensaumples yow beforn?
> Se ye nat alle how they ben forsworn?
> Where sen ye oon, that he ne hath laft his leef,
> Or ben unkynde, or don hire som myscheef,
> Or piled hire, or bosted of his dede?
> Ye may as wel it sen, as ye may rede.
> (F, 1254–63)

This is borne out by the following events, but only because the poet turns Aeneas into a cad who becomes tired of his conquest and has never really been in earnest. The dream in which he receives the divine command to pursue his mission and follow his destiny is an invention concocted on the spot to excuse himself and there is no sense of a real conflict. Aeneas is simply a traitor who leaves his lady to seek new adventures and to marry someone else. It is a complete distortion of Vergil's account, but it is done with so much genuine pathos and conviction that it is impossible to decide whether the narrator is completely in earnest or whether he knows that he has done injustice to the hero in the interest of his general theme.[21] There is no doubt

---

20. The first part of the legend is more elaborate and suggests something of the traditional stature of the characters. The second half returns to the more domestic tone of many of the other legends.

21. See Chaucer's earlier account of Dido's story in the *House of Fame*.

that Dido is domesticated and has lost some of her heroic stature. She begs Aeneas to make an honest woman of her by at least marrying her before killing her, and her suicide seems to be motivated by shame as much as by love. She even claims that she is with child, another pathetic detail Chaucer added to the story. It could, of course, like some other little hints, be interpreted in a less favourable way. Chaucer's female martyrs often seem to care for their status and their good name more than for more hidden values. Lucrece very primly covers her feet before expiring and although this detail is taken over from Ovid it seems a little more obtrusive and deliberate here:

> And as she fel adoun, she kaste hir lok,
> And of hir clothes yet she hede tok.
> For in hir fallynge yet she had a care,
> Lest that hir fet or suche thyng lay bare;
> So wel she loved clennesse and eke trouthe.
> (F, 1856–60)

Ariadne looks forward to becoming a duchess or even a queen when she is taken in by Theseus (F, 2123–35). Her legend is another instance of Chaucer reducing a potentially complex story to a simple tale of betrayal. Theseus is false from beginning to end and the narrator seems to fling the story into his face in order to expose him, rather than to extol the truth and steadfastness of the lady:

> Juge infernal, Mynos, of Crete kyng,
> Now cometh thy lot, now comestow on the ryng.
> Nat for thy sake oonly write I this storye,
> But for to clepe ageyn unto memorye
> Of Theseus the grete untrouthe of love;
> For which the goddes of the heven above
> Ben wrothe, and wreche han take for thy synne.
> Be red for shame! now I thy lyf begynne.
> (F, 1886–93)

The legend ends with a hearty curse: "the devel quyte hym his while!" (F, 2227). The "Legend of Phyllis" shows that his son is no better; he is another ungrateful cad, come ashore in great distress, received hospitably by a trusting woman whom he leaves ignominiously to her lone fate in the end. The narrator cannot keep back his indignation for long: he confesses that it wearies him to write about faithless lovers. The tone of this legend is not, it seems to me, consciously mocking or ironic, but rather naively trite. If "Chaucer is concerned to keep her (Phyllis) from our sympathies",[22] he does it indirectly,

22. Frank, p. 152.

by adopting a deliberately simple manner and a righteous anger not really justified by any real pathos. Phyllis is only one of a whole series of unsuspecting women and her fate is too common to be really tragic. The narrator's efforts to arouse our pity sound a little perfunctory, and he is not really moved by Phyllis' plight because her folly seems almost as glaring as the man's falsehood. There is no sustained attempt to turn her into a tragic figure although we are very far from *fabliau* territory.[23]

At the end the narrator mockingly presents himself as the only trustworthy lover: "trusteth, as in love, no man but me" (F, 2561). It is clear that he cannot take the tale or the telling of it entirely seriously, but by this very attitude he raises a number of interesting poetological questions. The uncertainty of tone is, at any rate, no sign of incompetence, but rather a sophisticated reflection on the relation between the poet and his subject-matter, a provocation or at least an invitation to think about traditional stories and outworn clichés. Mere repetition of the same story-patterns is not enough; by variations in tone, rhetorical artifice and point of view the reader is alerted to the arbitrary nature of literary tradition and fame.

Similarly abrupt changes in tone and seriousness can be found in several legends. At the end of the "Legend of Philomela" the narrator tells us that all men are wicked, even if they have not the courage to be as blatantly abhorrent as Tereus:

> Ye may be war of men, if that yow liste.
> For al be it that he wol nat, for shame,
> Don as Tereus, to lese his name,
> Ne serve yow as a morderour or a knave,
> Ful lytel while shal ye trewe hym have —
> That wol I seyn, al were ho now my brother —
> But it so be that he may have non other.
> (F, 2387–93)

These last lines mark a sudden decline from elevated pathos to a rather trite piece of everyday experience and to a world of petty rather than heroic wickedness. If we assume that Chaucer meant his readers to recognize the deliberate pruning of the Ovidian story this would again suggest that we are intended to see through the touching naïveté or exasperation of the narrator who turns every woman whose story he comes across into a pitiful martyr, at the cost even of half her vitality and spirit.

23. *Pace* Frank, p. 155. It is, of course, possible that Chaucer's contemporaries found more genuine tragic pathos in Phyllis' complaint, and readers may well differ as to the degree of subversive irony in Chaucer's account.

The last legend, and indeed the whole collection, ends without a proper conclusion. The transmission of texts is a precarious process, and there are many possible reasons why the versions that have come down to us should end at this particular point,[24] yet it seems rather appropriate that a story that is so particularly empty of genuine pathos and leaves so little room for any interesting development should be left without an elaborate ending. It is, of course, tempting to assume that Chaucer stopped his narrator deliberately to make clear that there was really no more to say. He can hardly have been unaware of the fact that in its present form, the "Legend of Hypermnestra" will not move many readers to genuine compassion and sympathy; the poor heroine is so weak and her dilemma so artificial that it would be difficult to make a real tragedy out of it. By reducing the situation to its bare outlines and toning down the whole narrative, Chaucer leaves the reader rather with fragments of a potential legend than with the complete story and this might well make him suspect that the narrator has lost interest. What conclusion should we expect?

Several generations of scholars after W.W. Skeat were convinced that Chaucer grew bored with the monotony of his legends and plodded on for nine tales with growing dissatisfaction until he gave up altogether. This is to take a rather simple and anachronistic view of the medieval poet and to introduce modern prejudices that do not seem to have occurred to any reader between the fifteenth and the nineteenth centuries. We are, to be sure, faced with the fact that Chaucer did not finish his collection of stories as he originally planned it, unless all the manuscripts of the completed work have been lost, which is at least a possibility: "The fact that the end has not survived is no proof that it was never written."[25]

John Lydgate's famous statement about Chaucer's collection seems to suggest, however, that he, only a generation or so after Chaucer, thought of the collection as unfinished:

> This poete wrot, at request off the queen,
> A legende off parfit hoolynesse,
> Off Goode Women to fynde out nynteen
> That dede excelle in bounte and fairnesse;
> But for his labour and (his) bisynesse
> Was inportable his wittis to encoumbre,
> In al this world to fynde so gret a noumbre.
> (Prologue to the *Fall of Princes*, 330—6).

24. See N.F. Blake, "Geoffrey Chaucer: the Critics and the Canon" *Archiv*, 211 (1984), 65—79.
25. Blake, p. 73. See also the very sane and balanced discussion by Frank, pp. 189—210 ("The Legend of Chaucer's Boredom"). Frank also quotes the passage from Lydgate.

The reason given by Lydgate is clearly facetious and may well be an indication that he did not quite know what to make of the collection, but there is no insinuation whatever to the effect that Chaucer got tired of his subject. It is clear from the text, I think, that Chaucer was aware of the narrow scope of his theme, and the fact that he emphasizes rather than modifies this narrowness proves that he wants to make the reader conscious of it. There is no noticeable attempt to make the stories different from each other in their uniform subject; on the contrary, the theme of female martyrdom and male treachery is repeated and insisted on to such an extent that the sameness must be part of the whole plan.[26] One single look at the *Canterbury Tales* should be enough to make clear that Chaucer was very much alive to the possibility of various, even mutually contradictory tales and narrative stances, and it is hardly possible that the poet who invented the Canterbury pilgrims should have failed to notice the glaring limitations of the *Legend* in this respect. This does not mean, however, that he got bored or did not think the whole project worth his while. He must have known many similar collections of rather uniform tales, like saints' legends, animal fables, *exempla*, or even Ovid's *Heroides* themselves. If the text reveals signs of a certain exasperation or at least a mild suggestion that all these legends of suffering women might be too much of a good thing, this is not Chaucer the poet getting bored, but rather Chaucer's narrator finding himself unable to fulfil his imposed task. Lydgate's not very original joke should not be taken too seriously, but at least, the first reader whose reaction has come down to us comments on the fragmentary character of the collection and wants to make us wonder whether anything was wrong with the subject or the treatment of it. In other words, Chaucer, as he does so often, passes the problem of the poet on to the reader and leaves him to reflect on the difficulties of literary composition.

There is no doubt that Chaucer was deeply impressed and influenced by Ovid's narrative brilliance, and the story-material provided by the *Metamorphoses*, the *Heroides*, and the *Fasti*, among others, had a strong appeal to him. He may well have felt that the challenge to retell these classical stories adequately in English was too much for him, and his narrator, evidently not quite capable of coping with the royal command, may be seen as an expression of

26. This is not to deny, however, that there are significant differences in style and narrative technique as well as in emphasis and degrees of seriousness, but the task imposed on the narrator makes, almost inevitably, for a certain monotony which Chaucer does not go out of his way to disguise.

his diffidence and modesty.[27] Even if he has not quite done justice to the
time-honoured classical myths there is no impression of pretentious failure
because the narrative method makes us share in the poet's struggle with his
subject and appreciate his genuine achievement. The ancient stories are re-
told in such a personal and unexpected way that they come to life by the
very process of presentation and interpretation.

It was one of Chaucer's earliest readers who recognized that there is a close
connection between his literary programme and his characterization of
women. About a century after Chaucer's death, Gavin Douglas, in the
prologue to his translation of the *Aeneid*, accuses Chaucer of deliberately
falsifying Vergil's account by blaming Aeneas for his part in the Dido story.
He excuses the poet with the famous dictum, "he was evir (God wait) all
womanis frend".[28] This explanation seems a little surprising at first because
reading the *Legend* critically it is difficult to believe that it was Chaucer's
chief purpose to take the part of poor forsaken women. It would be even
more misguided, however, to take the whole collection as a consistent parody of traditional complaint literature. It is true that the poet has drawn a
strikingly one-sided picture of loving women, in which credulity, truth and
a passive capacity for suffering are the predominant traits, but this directs
our attention to an important area of female experience and one quite different from that usually singled out in courtly love-poetry. The whole subject of the collection by no means contradicts Douglas' view of Chaucer as
"all womanis frend", if we do not understand this in the same simple and
superficial way as the God of Love. It is quite clear from the text that Chaucer does not write for readers who see nothing but the surface of the action
and the poet's professions, but expects us to appreciate the whole work as
a complex structure in which plot, frame, rhetoric and overall design all work
together to produce an effect that it is impossible to reduce to a simple moral. The elegiac pathos of the tales is as important as its mild subversion by
the poet's exaggerated obedience to Cupid's rather questionable command,
and his wholesale praise of women cannot be seen without a clear recognition
of its limitations, suggested by the God of Love's narrow views on literature.
It is in the critical examination of traditional clichés, be they literary or anti-

27. Kiser is, perhaps, overstating her case when she summarizes "Chaucer juxtaposes
    'good' poetry with 'bad' because he wishes to convey to us that he is serving two
    masters in the *Legend* – both Ovid and the God of Love" (p. 146), but she has
    certainly put her finger on the central problem.
28. *The Aeneid*, Book I, 449, quoted from *Selections from Gavin Douglas*, ed. D.F.C.
    Coldwell, *Clarendon Medieval and Tudor Series* (Oxford, 1964).

154

feminist, that Chaucer shows himself to be "womanis frend" because he refuses to identify himself either with naive idealization or with conventional anti-feminism. The form of the framed story collection seems particularly suited to his purpose because it enables him to present extreme views and simplified ideas in quotation marks and to discuss at the same time the problem of literary transmission. Chaucer's versions of the classical stories are an example of creative translation and a most original contribution to the valuable repository of books celebrated in the prologue as the key of remembrance. The poet's conviction that we ought to believe in old books does evidently not imply mere copying and blind faith, but critical debate and individual reflection. This is, of course, demonstrated with more gusto and sophistication in the *Canterbury Tales*, but there is no doubt that the *Legend of Good Women* is concerned with the same literary problem and in this sense it is indeed a kind of preparation for the more famous collection.[29]

A slightly revised version of this lecture appears as Chapter 7 of my book *Geoffrey Chaucer: an introduction to his narrative poetry* (Cambridge, 1986). My thanks are due to Cambridge University Press for permission to reprint the chapter here.